Backyard Self-sufficiency

Jackie French

Aird Books
Melbourne

Aird Books Pty Ltd
PO Box 122
Flemington, Vic. 3031
Phone (03) 9376 4461

First published by Aird Books in 1992
Reprinted February 1993
Reprinted October 1993
Reprinted December 1994
Reprinted April 1997
Reprinted July 1999

National Library of Australia
Cataloguing-in-publication data

French, Jacqueline
    Backyard self-sufficiency.

    Includes index.
    ISBN 0 947214 24 0

    1. Gardening–Australia. [2.] Self-sufficiency. I. Title.
635.0994

Cover design and illustrations by Lin Tobias
Text design by Lauren Statham
Typeset by Aird Books and Asset Type,
    South Melbourne, Victoria
Printed by Australian Print Group, Maryborough,
Victoria

Contents

*To Bryan, without whom this book and much else
could not have been written.
To Edward, a dedicated hunter-gatherer.
To everyone with dirty fingers who loves
and grows things.*

Introduction

Once upon a time . . .

When I was a child we lived in a new subdivision. Around us were neat gardens with shrubs and lawns, a small vegie garden or a few fruit trees.

Except next door. Mr Doo lived next door. He was one of the last Chinese market gardeners of the area. Like us, he had only a quarter acre. Unlike us, he used it all: thick, clipped rows of trees and wide banks of vegetables, so closely planted it was hard to tell the celery from the cabbages; banks of edible chrysanthemums and tall, red-flowered vines on poles that dripped with beans. Mr Doo made his living on the same ground that provided us with a few roses, a sandpit and a lot of lawn to mow on Sundays, and he had enough to give away as well.

Years later I learnt the old Australian ideal of self-sufficiency from our next-door neighbour. Jean learnt self-sufficiency many decades ago – but it wasn't called self-sufficiency then. It was just what everyone did in the Depression, when money was short, supermarkets unheard of, and the nearest shop a day's journey away.

I remember my first dinner at Jean's. A roast chook – an Indian game, small and sweet – with the chicken taste I'd forgotten from my childhood. (Today's frozen birds and even most free-range ones don't taste of much at all.) Potatoes, carrots, sweet potatoes, two sorts of beans and a small golden beetroot, all from the garden. Raspberries and cream for dessert – and through the window you could see the cow that gave the cream, chomping up the hill.

It was sponge cake for supper, made with duck eggs, with home-grown passionfruit on top, and home-made raspberry jam and more of Sally's cream. Of the whole meal, only a little flour and sugar were not home-grown.

Lunch was salad from the garden, and home-made cottage cheese. Breakfast was a soft-boiled egg and toast. Jean shopped only once a month. Apart from the cow (and in small areas you can substitute a goat) everything was grown on a plot as small as a normal suburban garden, and tended by a woman in her seventies.

In many countries a quarter acre is regarded as a lot of land. Most Australians waste their garden. A backyard should be able to feed you, entertain you, and give you joy – a good garden should be as thick as a fulfilled life. A self-sufficient garden need not mean digging up the dahlias and putting the lawn down to potatoes. It just needs planning.

Almost self-sufficient

I grow things because I enjoy it. The garden bulges with too many lettuces, radishes and parsnips, the apples are crowded into the mulberries, and the strawberries are rambling through everything so it is lucky the birds and wombats like them too.

I like having too much of everything. Maybe it's a siege mentality left over from my ancestors – when you never knew if you had to survive war or plague – or maybe it's just going through a winter with no supermarkets, cans or freeze-dried peas.

There's a difference, though, between growing most of what you eat and growing everything. It is easy to grow most of your fruit and vegetables on about a quarter acre – at least, it's easy once you get into the swing of it. It is almost as easy to grow most of your own tea, mustard, herbs and spices. But it's much, much harder to produce everything.

For a while my son and I were almost completely self-sufficient in food and a few staples. This was from necessity, not from choice. My income paid for petrol and preschool, but not much else. We lived and ate quite well. But I was glad when it was over.

Self-sufficiency is as insular as it is exhausting. You turn in on yourself. And there is little leeway for a crisis.

During that time I got pneumonia. It's even harder to be self-sufficient when you're ill. Friends may be willing to help – but while neighbours a hundred years ago might have harvested your apples and collected your eggs, nowadays they are more likely to expect to pick up your groceries for you. Neither the vegetable garden nor the orchard need much work, but we have to pick the food and then prepare it.

I began to long for canned tomatoes, lettuce that didn't have to be washed, and potatoes ready-washed.

It is harvesting that's most work in self-sufficiency. Growing nearly everything is easy. It is the final jump that's the trouble.

I'll probably never make our own soap again. But I'm glad to know I can do it. Anyway, you can buy lovely home-made soap in Braidwood (the town closest to our farm), and I'll cherish that instead. I'll buy Sandy's pots and Robyn's rugs and Peter's honey, and let someone else do the milking. The knowledge is still there to do those things myself, should I need to. But now I choose the jobs with which I fill my life.

Having gone through the experience myself, I have just this advice for those who want to be *totally* self-sufficient: don't do it. 'Almost self-sufficiency', though, can make your life as rich and prolific as your garden. Which bits you choose is up to you.

How much work is 'almost self-sufficiency'?

Most of us don't have time to tend a garden, to nurture it and coax it along. Luckily you don't have to break your back or commit your Sunday afternoons to it in order to grow most of your own food.

Our garden provides most of our fruit and vegetables. Apart from the picking, it gets roughly half an hour's work a week, including mowing the lawn. Through most of winter it doesn't even get this – and many weeks will go by when we don't do any work in the garden at all.

Of course it is a mess. But it's a productive mess and, I think, a beautiful mess. If we left, and returned in a hundred years it would still be providing food. It is a system that has been set up to feed us – and many other species – with a minimum of work, and a maximum of productivity and beauty.

How do we do it?

Plant thickly, with productive perennial species, and with many annuals that re-seed themselves. This is the first point. Most gardens are badly under-planted. Thicker planting not only means you fit more in: it means that weeds can't enter; that the ground is covered with greenery and doesn't dry out as fast; and that accumulated 'wastes' and the bacteria associated with nitrogen-fixers – like clover, broom, wattles, lupins, casaurinas and the sweet peas that clamber through the trees – add organic matter to the soil.

We've got strawberries under fruit trees, 'wild' potato beds, garlic patches that grow themselves, and indestructible providers like chokos and Jerusalem artichokes and foliage turnips and hops and banana passionfruit. They are healthy plants in healthy, fertile soil. This is the second point. *Healthy plants need less work.*

To have healthy plants you need healthy soil. Ours used not to be: it was so worked out that even grass wouldn't grow. But we mulched, and grew green-manure crops (plants grown just to be slashed to rot back into the soil), and added hen manure and other organic matter – and now the soil is rich and black.

We don't use pesticides either. Why bother? We grow flowering shrubs and let vegetables go to seed, and both attract predators to do our pest control for us. And we grow so much that a little loss doesn't matter. We don't use herbicides either, except for testing. Every plant has a use – even if it's just to be dug up to make compost or liquid manure.

We use 'no-dig', low-work gardens, which need a minimum of maintenance from year to year (see Chapter 3). This is the third point: *the more you interfere with nature, the more you have to maintain.* A wombat track doesn't need maintenance, but a bitumen road does. The more you weed your garden, the more weeds appear in the bare ground. The more you prune your trees the more you have to prune the lush new growth – and the more you have to feed them to make up for the prunings you've taken.

No-one maintains the bush, but it keeps on feeding countless species. Once you establish a self-sufficient system it should keep feeding you . . . and feeding you . . . and keep growing in productivity and beauty.

Why grow your own?

I like growing our food. It makes life richer. If you buy potatoes from the supermarket that's all you get: potatoes. But for me, this evening's spuds give memories too: grubbing them up with Edward this morning, and listening to the lyrebird sing, and smelling the soft, damp soil. I remember Bryan mulching them with the wild oats he'd mown in the asparagus patch (whilst accidentally mowing the asparagus too). I remember when the spuds were first planted, years ago, and Mrs Hobbins down the road showed me how to bandicoot them so you always had a crop. There are a million memories associated with those potatoes. There is something deeply satisfying in working with life's necessities: crops and shelter, children, other species.

There are other reasons, too, for growing your own. There is the knowledge that, as a household, we did not contribute to the Bhopal disaster, or to any other tragedy associated with making pesticides for the wealthy. We don't support the fertiliser industry either: our fertility is home-grown or scavenged. And if it relied on people like us, the food-processing industry would go bust.

Every one of us, I think, has a little of our ancestors' 'siege mentality': a need to fill the cupboards and bolt the door. Growing your own is the best security you can have. It means your food is always fresh and unpolluted. It means you never have to worry about the cost of fruit and vegetables. (This year we fed most of our late peaches to the chooks – our friends were sick of them, and so were we. Strawberries? I haven't bothered picking them for weeks. And as for beans, I think my family would go on strike if they were given the hard, stringy things or – worse – the watery, frozen slips of green plastic you buy in shops. They like butter beans, or young five-penny beans, or new purple kings . . .

For us it's true wealth to give away the kiwi fruit, to press our limes on satiated friends, to take armfuls of daffodils up to town to celebrate the spring, and baskets full of roses all through summer. Our standard of living is far higher than anyone on our sort of income could normally expect, because we produce things that we would otherwise have to buy, and because many of the joys in our lives – like being surrounded by flowers

and watching birds splutter in the fountain – are things we don't have to pay for.

Anyone who has ever watched a child's face as they fill a basket of oranges, or as they disappear for an hour in the raspberry beds, or as they watch the progress of a seed as it becomes a vine and sprouts large melons, then let them pick it – all their own work – will know there is something very basic and very good about growing your own. This is after all what life's about: food and shelter, life and death, and growing things. There is no better place than a garden for maintaining contact with these basic things.

I, like all humans, am part of the earth. To work it, watch it, live within its rhythms – for me, that is the deepest satisfaction.

Conclusion

It was afternoon tea, and we were the youngest there. They were reminiscing, about the days of plenty – buckets full each year. Walnuts that you ate as fast as they were cracked, chestnuts by the sackful, cherries that went through a seeder so you crammed them in in handfuls, grapes by the basketful. Yet this was a time when money was short: shirts made out of old flour sacks, and patchwork skirts – from need, not fashion.

The writer Norman Douglas once said: 'To be miserly towards your friends is not pretty; to be miserly towards yourself is contemptible.' Yet, this is what we have today: an apple at lunch-time, floury and waxed, costing the better part of a dollar; peaches you buy individually because they cost so much; a kilo of grapes. I know families who, in the middle of our peach season, get more videos than peaches. Because peaches are 'too expensive'. But peaches cost nothing – if you grow them yourself!

I have two images of suburban life today.

The first is of a neat house set in a mown lawn with trimmed shrubs and a sandpit; a clean kitchen with yesterday's take-away containers on the sink; and the latest videos to fill your life after dinner.

The second is of a suburban jungle: a maze of tangled apple trees and grape vines, carpets of strawberries, and kids with mulberry-stained faces who don't come inside till dark. You trip over a box of apples in the laundry, and the kitchen smells of summer tomatoes and of the basil on the window sill.

The kitchen shelves are full, and so are the lives of the inhabitants.

The richness of our lives depends on our surroundings and what we fill them with.

Chapter 1

Planning the self-sufficient garden

Knowing what to plant

Few of us today really know what we eat. This is because most of the food we eat is bought weekly – or even daily – as we need it, on impulse or near-impulse.

Getting to know your needs

How many people know how many potatoes they eat per year, or even per week; how many apples, how much parsley, how many bunches of grapes? Even adding together what you buy now won't necessarily tell you what you may decide to eat home-grown. Peaches are expensive in the shops, but we feed our home-grown surplus to our geese. That means we buy neither goose food nor any number of cheap alternatives to peaches-and-cream for dessert.

Leftover avocados, the harder bits of asparagus, and beetroot that get a bit shrivelled all go into the compost. In the self-sufficient garden nothing is wasted – because everything is recycled. What you don't eat goes to growing more, via the compost bin.

Home-grown means you can indulge your taste for luxury. It has taken me many years to work out what our family eats: how many broccoli plants we like, or brussels sprouts, how many artichokes, how many late peaches or early apricots. I've learnt what veg to plant near the kitchen door, for me to grab when it's raining or when I want to prepare a meal quickly. I've learnt when to expect visitors (like at Christmas and school holidays), and to plant my garden accordingly.

Looking at your garden

If you want a 'self-sufficient' garden you need to work out different ways of using space. I'm not advocating you dig up your roses or plant crops in the kids' sandpit. But nearly every garden has large areas that aren't used: the shady bit along the side, the awkward corner of the lawn where no-one plays, the unused ground below the trees, even the strips of lawn beneath the clothes line or up the drive. There are food-producing plants appropriate to all such areas.

Fences

Most fences don't grow anything. I hate naked fences. They look better green. Try:
• Perennial climbing beans – they'll come up every year and give you thick, wide beans you can eat young and tender or keep for 'dried' beans. They'll also cover your fence with greenery and bright red flowers.
• Chokos – eat the shoots as well as the fruit.
• Hops – hops die down in winter and ramble all over the place in summer. Eat the young shoots in early spring, make beer from the flowers, or use them to stuff hop pillows.
• Plant passionfruit in frost-free places, and banana passionfruit in cold areas.
• Loganberries, marionberries, boysenberries and other climbing berries can be trained up wire stapled to the fence.
• Grapes – there are hundreds of grape varieties in Australia, suitable for any area from snowy winters to tropical summers.
• Plant flowering climbers like clematis, wonga vine, perennial sweet peas, bougainvillea, jasmine, or rambling roses to attract birds, predaceous insects, and for pleasure.
• Edible Chinese convolvulus.
• Sweet potatoes, for temperate areas only.
• Or use your fence to stake up tomatoes, peas, or broad beans.

Fruit trees

The area next to the fence is the best for large fruit trees. Hedge your garden boundaries with tall fruit trees. Plant them 2 metres apart. They'll grow tall to reach the sun and the branches will tangle. This means birds won't find most of the fruit (though you will), and tall trees bear as much fruit as wide ones – you just have to climb the tree or use a fruit picker on a tall stick to get the crop. This way you'll be able to have a far greater variety of fruit than with a normally planted orchard.

With close planting, a normal backyard block can have at least twenty fruit trees. The selection is up to you: it depends on what grows best in your area and what you like to eat. As a basic rule I'd suggest:
• three apples (late, early, and medium),

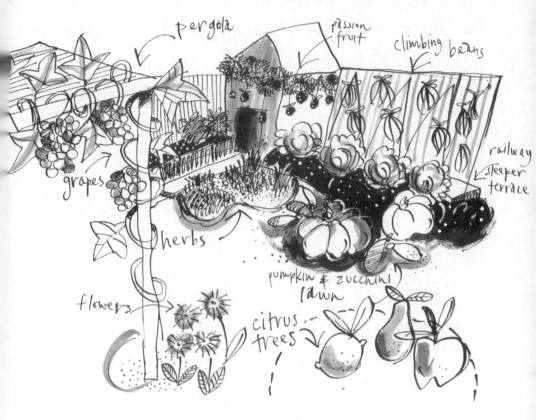

- one valencia and one navel orange (frost permitting),
- one lemon (in cold areas, try bush lemons or citronelles – the other trees will help shelter them from the frost),
- a loquat, for the earliest fruit,
- and the rest according to preference.

Remember that early and late varieties may be separated by three months or more. Two plums of the same variety may be too many for you to use if they crop at the same time, but a January ripener will be finished by the time late-season ones come in.

Plant dwarf fruit trees along paths as a hedge – dwarf apples, dwarf peaches, pomegranates or nectarines – or plant trees like hazelnuts that can be trimmed to a neat hedge.

Small fruit

Next to the trees plant 'small' fruit: raspberries, blueberries, tamarillos, pepino, pineapple, elder trees for flowers and berries, kumquats, guavas, strawberry guavas, or Chilean hazelnuts.

Most 'small' fruit is naturally an under-story crop anyway: they accept shade for at least part of the day. They will also cast much less shade over the next part of your garden. You can also plant 'small' fruit among the 'permanent' beds.

Permanent beds

These are the crops you plant once and harvest for the rest of your life. I think they're wonderful: a bit of mulching and they keep rewarding you. See Chapter 3, under 'The perennial vegetable garden' for advice on growing and use:

- Artichokes
- Asparagus
- Chicory
- Dandelions
- Ginger
- Kumeras
- Rhubarb
- Rocket
- Sorrel
- Sweet potatoes

Plants for out-of-the-way corners

Arrowroot

You can eat this like sweet potato, or grate it and wash out the starch for arrowroot thickener. It looks like a canna lily – and it is: *Canna edulis*, high as your waist and pretty.

Bamboo

Eat the shoots in spring: these fresh 'bamboo shoots' taste better than any out of a can. Slice them into boiling water and leave for ten minutes or until they are no longer bitter.

Horseradish

This is a good 'under-tree' crop. Plant a piece of root and it will ramble all over the moist ground. The leaves are also edible (like silverbeet), but a bit hot for most tastes.

Jerusalem artichokes

These are a form of sunflower with wonderful, tall colour in late summer. Plant a few and they'll multiply like the loaves and fishes and you'll never be rid of them. Dig up the tubers in autumn and bake them, boil them, fry them, or make them into a soup. Tasty, but gas producing!

Vegetable gardens

These will demand most work in your self-sufficient garden: they are annuals that need tending and re-planting. Actually, the 'permanent beds' will give you more than enough food. It's just that this does not include the staples we're used to, like tomatoes, potatoes and corn.

Plant your vegie garden in the sunniest place you have, to get the most vegies per square metre. I tend to have a 'basic' garden that I plant every year. It yields enough to keep us in most vegetables for most meals with very little work. Then, if I have time, I plant the 'luxuries'.

Basic crops include silverbeet (a dozen plants will give you most of your greens for a year), tomatoes and pumpkins (because they grow themselves), and broccoli (which can be planted once and harvested for the next year, as long as you pick it every day).

Vegetable gardens don't have to be a lot of work. See also Chapter 3, under 'Minimum work gardens' – gardens that take ten minutes to make and plant, and only ten minutes of work a week.

Consider 'indestructibles' like Chinese mustard, Chinese cabbage, Chinese celery and collards. These are all frost, heat, and drought-hardy greens, slightly tougher than their Aussie counterparts. Collards are like cabbage leaves, and you eat them the same way. They are slightly tougher, but very, very hardy and prolific.

If you really enjoy growing your own there is no reason why you shouldn't have a bed of rice or wheat. I have grown both in the backyard: one square metre will give you a bucketful. The taste is wonderful.

House walls

This is one of the most valuable areas of your garden. Brick or stone house walls store a lot of heat: you can use them as a micro-climate to grow fruit that may not survive in the open garden. Walled gardens are good too. We grow passionfruit on a pergola next to the walls here, bananas up the walls, and sweet potatoes, cardamom, and other frost-tender plants in a garden below them.

Plant espaliered fruit trees – heat-loving varieties – next to the heat-absorbing wall of your house. Put frost-tender ones like avocados and oranges facing north. This way, even many Tasmanian gardens can grow sub-tropical fruit!

Pergolas

Pergolas keep the house cool in summer. Look for deciduous bearers like grapes, kiwi fruit, perennial peas, chokos or hops. Consider passionfruit or pepper in hot areas.

Lawns

Look at your lawn, work out how much of it is used, then plant the rest. Let pumpkins wander over it; plant potatoes; fill up the edges with small fruit like pepino, brambleberries, raspberries, kumquats, or blueberries.

Under the clothes line

This is a low-use area, trodden on only when you hang out or bring in the washing. Surround the base of your clothes line with a couple of rosemary bushes or lavender (it will make the clothes smell all the sweeter), and pave underneath it, leaving lots of spaces for herbs like marjoram, oregano, chamomile and mints that don't mind being trodden on.

Shady areas

Under the trees, round the back and under the pergola, plant edible plants for shady areas. Many plants need shade or semi-shade, especially those that originated as under-story plants in forests. Don't grow grass in your shady areas: it will choke out the fruit. I grow violets there instead. Make use of shady spots with a ground cover of any of the following plants.

Asparagus

Asparagus tolerates semi-shade from a pergola above it, but not deep shade. I grow asparagus under the kiwi fruit. The asparagus bears in spring before the kiwi fruit come into leaf.

Blueberries

Blueberries tolerate light, but not deep shade. You can also plant them where they get morning sun and afternoon shade.

Cape gooseberries

These grow well under trees, especially in frosty areas where the trees give some protection.

Lettuce

In hot areas lettuce grows best under a pergola. Even in temperate areas lettuce tolerates light shade and will grow under trees like peach or almond which don't shade the ground completely.

Parsley

See lettuce. We grow parsley under the kiwi fruit – or rather it grows itself, re-seeding every year.

Sorrel

This is a leafy, slightly bitter green. Grow it under trees.

Strawberries

These are forest plants and grow best under trees. They are shallow-rooted and won't compete with tree roots. Make sure they have plenty of phosphorous.

Growing upwards

Even in a very small garden you can 'borrow' space by growing upwards. Put up trellises and grow vegetables vertically instead of horizontally. Wherever possible I grow climbing varieties. They take up less room, and you only need to weed the small area at the base of the trellis. We grow climbing tomatoes, beans and peas as well as the standard cucumbers and melons.

Consider window boxes. Stick poles in the middle of the garden, for grapevines or chokos or passionfruit to wander up. They don't have to be spread out: a ten-foot pole gives a lot of grapes and takes almost no room. You can also grow passionfruit or grapevines through your trees.

Make terraces for flowers, vegetables, and small fruit like gooseberries and raspberries. Terraces give you much more planting space than flat ground. You can make terraces with railway sleepers or bricks or rocks, or even old tyres scavenged from the local garage. Build them as high as you can be bothered: the more tiers the more space.

Three-tier planting

What I've described above is a classic peasant garden. Peasant gardens are 'three-tier' gardens: a framework of trees with small bushes and low crops between them. The third tier consists of animals: chooks, ducks, rabbits, guinea pigs, geese, and guinea fowl (see chapter 7).

Re-think all unused space. Plant the drive with strawberries: you'll squash a few berries sometimes, but that's better than no harvest at all. Plant out the nature strip (preferably with plants that passers by won't recognise as edible, and pinch): tea camellias, loquats, medlars, pomegranates, japonica (make jam or stewed fruit), Irish strawberries, guavas, hibiscus, kurrajong, elderberries, oaks (acorns for hen food), jojoba, white mulberries, or bamboo (for shoots).

Even a small backyard should be able to grow some forty trees, thousands of strawberry plants, several dozen berry bushes, climbing berries and a good number of fruiting shrubs.

Self-sufficient gardens are beautiful: a ramble of productivity, a profusion of smells and colour. We've forgotten how beautiful edible plants can be: fat, red apples and tendrils of grapes, bountiful chokos and soft feathery fennel, the wide, bright blooms of passionfruit, the scent of orange blossom on a summer night. It's like a Garden of Eden in your own backyard.

Chapter 2

Growing staples

On either side the river lie,
Long fields of barley and of rye . . .
But our small crop is ripe, you see
Over by the apple tree
[with apologies to The Lady of Shallott . . .]

Your own grains, beans and lentils, sugars and oils

Even green-fingered gardeners (the sort who give away buckets of tomatoes every summer and have flowers when the rest of the world is dead) rarely grow their own staple crops like wheat or oil, or potatoes even. This may be because staples are cheap and often need processing, while you are unlikely to be able to grow all your family needs in the backyard. But you can, in fact, make a big contribution.

A little extra work will give you enough dried beans for storage, in addition to fresh ones. If you don't use much sugar it is possible to grow all you need, especially if you use other home-grown sweeteners too.

Even a small patch of sunflowers, or an olive or walnut tree will provide you with oil for a good part of the year at least. Again, it depends of course on how much oil you use.

Even a few square metres under oats, repeatedly cropped, will probably keep your family in porridge, if you don't eat it every day. And while the average home garden probably can't produce enough wheat for a permanent supply, a slightly larger garden certainly can. A well-fertilised wheat patch should return at least half a kilo of wheat per square metre – possibly more, as the greater care and preparation you can give a small area means your yields will be much greater than commercial ones.

But even if you can't produce a whole year's supply, it is still worthwhile growing a small quantity of wheat – for the sheer enjoyment of growing something different, to have fresh, whole grains for cooking (you can substitute whole wheat for rice in any recipe as long as you double the cooking time), or to crack it for tabouli, and so on.

Fresh, home-grown grains, oils and potatoes have the same relationship to their bought cousins as a home-grown tomato has to the pale, artificially ripened, commercial specimens. Gardeners are connoisseurs of fresh vegetables. Fresh grain is just as wonderful as fresh vegetables. Home-pressed oil still tastes of the sun. Home-grown spuds are like nothing you've ever bought in a shop – and even home-made sugar is fun.

Finding seed

Seeds can be ordered from Stock & Station agents (listed as such in the Yellow Pages), or through a helpful nursery which might order it in for you. Fresh, unprocessed seed from health-food stores will often germinate. The best mail-order suppliers I know for small amounts of grain seed are:
• Eden Seeds, the Finch Family, M.S. 316, Gympie, Queensland 4570, and
• Phoenix Seeds, PO Box 207, Snug, Tasmania 7154.

Grains

For a good crop, most grains need soil which is rich in nitrogen and phosphorous – though you will give usually get some crop on almost any soil. Some, like millet, rye and buckwheat will tolerate much harsher conditions than wheat.

Plant all grains thickly, scattering the seed by hand so there is no more than a couple of centimetres between each grain. Home-grown grain should be planted much closer together than commercial grain, firstly because the ground is probably in better condition, but also because in a small area thickly planted grain is less likely to 'lodge' or fall over.

The extra water and fertilisation you can give a small area will compensate for thick sowing.

The harvesting, processing and storing techniques for wheat can be applied to any grain. Always make sure though that your grain is dry and stays dry: never store damp grain, and never use grain that looks or smells mouldy.

Most grain seed can be easily obtained by buying whole untreated seed for consumption from health-food shops. Choose the freshest you can get, and test it before you plant it by soaking it in water. If the grain floats it won't germinate. Grain intended for stock food, like hen food or stud mix, is another cheap way of getting 'staple' seed. Most Stock & Station agents will sell small quantities, though some may try to sell you only by the bag full.

Barley

Barley prefers a neutral soil with only moderate humus content to prevent lodging. If your soil is acid you must add lime, wood ash or dolomite for a good crop. Sow barley at about 4 g per square metre, raking it in to about 2 cm deep. It is a fast-growing crop, usually sown in April or July. I buy 'hull-less' barley seed from Phoenix Seeds.

Barley mushrooms and asparagus

Take three cups of finely chopped mushrooms, onions, garlic and asparagus. Add a cup of barley. Seethe the lot in two tablespoons of butter for as long as you can be bothered, but at least twenty minutes. Now add some stock or water – the exact quantity will depend on the absorbency of your barley. Start with three cups of liquid and be prepared to add more. Add a dash of soy sauce.

Place a heavy lid on your pot, and cook as slowly as possible until all the liquid has been absorbed. If the grain is still hard, add more liquid and keep cooking until it is soft. Serve hot.

Buckwheat

This can be grown on any poor ground and is very useful as a 'reclaiming' crop, to be slashed or dug in as a green manure. It is said to make phosphorous in the soil more available for other plants and is an excellent forage for bees.

Sow buckwheat in late spring, at about 8 g per square metre. It matures in about 70 days and does best in cool, wet climates, though it can be grown almost anywhere. I have grown it on almost pure clay during a drought. There wasn't much to harvest – but a harvest there was. You can harvest buckwheat by shaking out the seeds; it doesn't need hulling.

Try cracking the grain, soaking it overnight and making it into porridge. Buckwheat can be cooked like rice; it can be added to rice dishes to give them more flavour; or it can be ground into flour. Russian buckwheat pancakes or *blini* are traditionally made with buckwheat flour.

Blini

Mix a cup of buckwheat flour with a cup of plain flour. Add a beaten egg and a cup and a half of milk. Blend well. Drop spoonfuls of the batter onto a greased frying pan. Fry them until golden, then turn them. Eat them with caviar and sour cream, with cherry jam, or simply with sugar and lemon juice.

Maize

Maize is grown the same way as sweet corn, but the yields are much greater and the stalks will grow up to twice your height. Some varieties of maize will produce up to six cobs per stalk. Maize is a very heavy feeder: the more you feed your maize, the higher the yield.

You can eat maize when it is young and tender, before the cob 'yellows' all the way up. After that it becomes tough and floury: feed it to the hens or other stock, or grind it to make cornflour or rough-ground polenta. Dried maize kernels are also good added to long-cooking stews, to thicken them. But make sure they get at least two hours' cooking.

If you wish to store your maize on the stalk until you need it, simply bend the stalk over to cover the cob and to prevent rain damage. Otherwise, pick it when the stalks are brown and the grain is quite hard.

There are several sorts of maize available in Australia. The one sold mostly for stock food is edible, though not as good as the others. The red-kerneled varieties make better eating, especially when young. I find Phoenix Seeds and Eden Seeds the best suppliers of unusual varieties that grow true to type from your own seed (see p xx).

Millet

Millet is a fast growing, annual summer grass. It grows up to one metre high, has small seeds, and matures in 45 to 90 days. It tolerates very poor soil, though yields are far greater on good land.

Millet should be sown in early summer and be well-watered: it is not at all drought tolerant, and will be killed by the first frost. Make sure the seed bed is well prepared when you sow millet, as the seeds are very small. Sow them about 2 to 3 cm deep, preferably on fairly fertile soil with adequate nitrogen and phosphorous, if possible.

Millet can be ground to add to flour, made into a porridge or boiled like rice (but for twice as long) and served in the same manner. However, millet is a starvation food: easily grown in poor conditions, but far less tasty then any of the alternatives. In Australia it is mostly grown for canary seed (this is one way of getting millet seed for sowing), but in some parts of Asia and Africa it is used for human consumption, usually to make bread, cakes or millet porridge.

Oats

Oats can tolerate a more acid soil than wheat, need less moisture and can be sown on rougher ground. They like a humus-rich soil and plenty of nitrogen and phosphorous.

Oats should be sown at about 12 g per square metre and raked in until the seeds are about 2.5 cm deep.

Oats can be sown either in autumn or spring, though autumn sowing is more usual. Spring crops have a fairly high water requirement. You can harvest oats as soon as the grains begin to harden on the outside (*see* wheat). Oats are prone to 'shatter', so harvesting should not be delayed.

Oat flour can be added to wheat flour. Three parts wheat to one part oat flour makes a tasty bread. A half-and-half mixture can be used for biscuits and slices.

Rice

There are two main types of rice grown commercially, *Oryza sativa indica* and *Oryza sativa japonica*.

Indica is a long, hard-grained rice, best suited to tropical areas. Japonica is higher yielding, with short, soft grains. It adapts well to temperate areas. New cultivars have blurred the clear distinction between the two, but most rice grown in Australia is short-grain, soft rice. Rice is mostly used for human consumption, though it can be fed to stock. The hulls can be used for absorbent packing or pressed for edible rice oil.

If you can grow oranges in your area you can probably also grow rice. To grow rice in the home garden, 'trench' up an area so it will hold water, at least overnight. This is best done by digging a 20 cm deep pit, or by hilling up an area so the banks are about 15 cm high and lining the edges with a thick layer of old newspapers.

Rice needs a reasonably high nitrogen level – apply it before the rice is planted – but low levels of phosphorous. Sow the rice 1 to 3 cm deep in late September to early October. Keep the area well watered, but not flooded, until the plants are well established, then flood them to between 5 and 15 cm deep. Keep the area flooded with a trickling hose until the grain is nearly ready. It isn't disastrous if it dries out occasionally, especially overnight, but try to keep the water level up.

An alternative method of growing is to germinate the seed on wet cotton wool, then broadcast it over an area that has already been shallowly flooded.

Rice is sometimes grown for home quantities without flooding, though it must always be kept moist and completely weed-free. Plant it very thickly to keep up the humidity and to stop it from falling over. Mulch it deeply, and always keep the mulch damp.

As the rice ripens the panicle swells and becomes golden brown. Drain the rice at this stage, then wait a further three weeks or so till the grain is ready. Test it by breaking some open.

Once the rice is shaken off the stalks it must be hulled. This can be done at home by rubbing it through a sieve, or by rubbing the grain through your fingers then turning a fan on it so the light hulls blow away. You now have brown rice, still with its high-vitamin oil-rich germ, but with keeping qualities inferior to white rice. To get white rice, further polishing is needed to remove the outer coats of the kernel. This is difficult to do at home.

Rye

Rye is usually referred to as 'rye corn' or 'rye cereal' to distinguish it from rye-grass. Rye can be grown on extremely poor soil and will survive much colder conditions than wheat or oats. Rye also needs little moisture and is less prone to insect damage than other grains. On the other hand, yields are usually smaller than for the other grains.

Rye is normally sown in March or April. It should be harvested when the seeds are dry and hard, and drop easily from the heads. You need to be especially careful that rye is kept dry and doesn't go mouldy.

Rye is usually made into flour. It is less responsive to yeast than wheat, and makes a heavier bread. However, a small proportion of rye added to breads, pancakes and even fruit cakes gives them a richer flavour.

Triticale

This is a wheat/rye cross, very high-yielding, and high in protein and various amino acids. It can be grown wherever wheat is grown. Triticale flour is better than rye, but not as good as wheat for high-rising bread. It can also be made into cakes and pancakes, breakfast cereals, and wonderful unleavened chappattis. Unless you like rich, heavy bread triticale is best used mixed with wheat flour, or where no leavening is needed.

Wheat

Wheats are either spring or winter types. Winter wheat needs a period of low temperature to develop flowering heads. It is usually planted in autumn. It is usually a 'hard' high-protein wheat, high in gluten. A high-gluten wheat makes the best bread; a low-gluten wheat makes better cakes, and gives the best results when yeast isn't needed.

Most Australian wheat is spring wheat, 'soft' low-gluten wheat useful for cakes and pastry. In mild areas, spring wheat can also be grown in autumn and winter. In fact, spring wheat can be sown at almost any time of the year, although most wheat is sown between April and June, and sometimes as early as February. However, wheat sown in spring may be damaged by early frost.

If wheat is sown in April you should harvest it in about November, but the time will vary according to the type of wheat and the warmth of the season, and cool areas won't have their harvest until February.

Wheat needs a medium to heavy soil with a neutral pH, high in phosphorous and nitrogen. It is usually grown where rainfall averages 400 to 1000 mm a year.

Sow wheat at 4 to 5 g per square metre, about 4 cm deep. It is usually sown in rows about 18 cm apart, but in a small area it is best sown as an amorphous block to stop 'lodging' or falling over.

Keep the soil moist until the wheat has germinated and water it regularly till the grain starts to swell. At that stage, dryer conditions will give a better quality wheat.

If you have chickens or other animals, you can put them to graze on the young wheat before it starts to head. This will both provide stock food, add manure and urine to the wheat, and promote more 'heads' – i.e. more grain.

Your wheat is ready to harvest when the plants look yellow, with still a few streaks of green in the stalks. By then you should be able to shake out the grain with a vigorous waving – but it should not be falling out of its own accord.

Chew a bit of the grain. If it is soft or milky it is still green, if it is hard and crunchy it is very ripe – and will probably 'shatter' when you try and harvest it by hand, causing you to lose most of the grain as you cut it. Combine harvesters can reap wheat at this stage, but for hand harvesting the wheat needs to be greener.

Try to pick your wheat when it is crunchy outside but still soft inside. Scythe down the wheat and tie it into bundles. Use a brushhook, a scythe or even garden shears to cut it, and tie it with a stalk of wheat or string.

Lean the bundles against each other, grain heads upwards. It must now be kept dry, so be prepared to cover it or take it into a shed if it looks like rain.

Leave the grain for about two weeks in cool weather; half that time or less in hot, dry conditions. It is ready when the grains fall out easily and taste hard and dry.

Now spread out an old sheet or tarpaulin and bash the bunches of wheat onto it. The grain will shatter from the heads. Then 'winnow' it to remove the husks and bits of chaff. A simple but unconventional winnowing method is to put the grain in a bucket and pour it out slowly in front of an electric fan or in a strong breeze, so that the lighter chaff blows away, and the heavy grain falls to the ground. Repeat this three or four times, until the grain is clean.

Another way is to place the grain on racks and gently rub it through wire mesh; or just let it gradually fall through itself. Or you can laboriously pick out the bits of chaff by hand.

Store the grain away from rodents in an airtight container with a few bay leaves and dried garlic cloves to repel weevils. (They won't taint the grain.) Another method is to light a candle in the middle of the container of grain just before you seal up the lid. When the candle has used up all the air it goes out, and the weevils can't survive.

To get the best baking quality, grind the grain just before you need it for cakes, or about ten days before you want to use it for bread. Fresh wheat and fresh flour tastes beautiful.

Wheat and mushroom soup
Fry a cup of chopped onions in butter, add two cups of field mushrooms, some chopped garlic, a touch of soy sauce, a cup of wheat, and enough stock to drown the lot. Simmer for an hour. Serve with a dash of sour cream or yoghurt.

Wheat pudding
Place a cup of wheat in an ovenproof dish, cover with a layer of sliced apple and some chopped dates. Sprinkle with cinnamon, add brown sugar to taste – a dessertspoon should be ample. Add one cup of cream and three cups of milk. Sprinkle with nutmeg. Place in a slow oven and leave till the liquid has been absorbed.

Wheat and vegetables
Seethe a cup of chopped vegetables – like celery, carrot, asparagus, beans, peas, onions, garlic, etc. – in butter until they are semi-cooked. Add a cup of wheat and four cups of stock. Put a lid on the pot and cook very slowly until

the liquid has been absorbed. If the wheat is still hard, add more stock. Don't stir at any stage or the wheat will become gluggy and may stick to the bottom.

Peas and beans

These are an excellent protein staple: easy to grow, and easy to dry and store, they'll keep for years. The bacteria associated with their roots will fix nitrogen from the air and return it to your garden.

Adzuki beans

These are also known as Japanese red beans. Buy the seed in Asian speciality shops. Most dried seed sold for cooking will germinate. Adzuki beans are an annual, grown like green beans, but they will withstand higher temperatures and drought. They need a frost-free period of between 3 and 5 months to grow to maturity. The beans should be left on the bush until they are dry. Then you can split them and take out the seeds, and dry them further for a couple of days before storing.

Adzuki beans can be cooked with rice, ground and used for bean paste, or dried for later use in stews. They can also be used like green beans, if picked immature.

Chick peas

Chick pea bushes are about half a metre high, with small feathery branchlets (these are poisonous) and leathery seed pods. Chick peas will grow wherever you grow other peas, but they need between 4 and 7 months for the pea pods to dry out and the seeds to reach maturity. Make sure the area is kept clear of weeds – chick peas can't stand much weed competition.

Plant chick peas bought from the supermarket, after soaking them overnight. If they float they won't germinate, so try and buy fresh packets.

Field or navy beans

These are the baked bean crop. They can be grown wherever other beans grow. Most navy beans are planted from November to February. They don't tolerate high temperatures, frost, or waterlogging. It takes a crop about 3 to 4 months to mature. They are heavy feeders, and susceptible to zinc deficiency.

Navy beans can be harvested as soon as they are big enough, and used fresh. Or they can be left until the pods are brittle, for drying and long keeping.

Green beans

Common, everyday, green, yellow, or red beans can be kept for drying. Just let the beans you can't use stay on the bushes until the pods are brittle and the beans large and hard. I have stored various varieties of green string beans in this way, and they have all been sweet and excellent when I used them.

Lab lab beans

Lab lab is a perennial twining herb, though it is usually planted as an annual. It will grow on poor or dry soil or any well drained land. It must be staked. Yields can be enormous, and in frost free areas lab lab beans will continue to crop for several years.

Lab lab beans can be grown in summer in cool and temperate areas and in winter in the tropics. Regular feeding and watering will increase yields.

Lab lab beans must be cooked: they are poisonous raw. The leaves can be cooked like silverbeet, the beans eaten like green beans, and the seed dried for use like split peas.

Pigeon peas

These can be perennial, tall-growing leguminous bushes, grown either from seed or cuttings. They are drought resistant, and will tolerate light frost. Prune them lightly every year after picking, to encourage new growth. Pigeon peas can be grown as a border around the garden where the rich prunings can be used as mulch.

Pigeon peas can be eaten fresh or they can be shelled, dried and stored. Cook them like ordinary peas by boiling or steaming them when fresh, or soaking and boiling them when dried. They are very high in protein and calcium.

Red lentils

These grow up to 40 cm high on a straggly vine. They need conditions similar to peas. The seeds can be sprouted from stock bought in health food stores.

Soybeans

These can be grown from the soybean seeds bought in supermarkets. They are very adaptable, have similar requirements to green beans, and taste very similar when picked young.

Pick the beans when they are still tender and eat them like green beans. Use them fresh and podded as soon as the beans are big enough, even though the pods are still green, or if you want to store them, leave the pods on the stalk until the whole plant is brittle.

Soybeans can be dried and ground into flour, or roasted in the oven like peanuts. I soak them overnight in water and honey, dry them, and fry them with garlic in oil till they are brown and crisp.

Soybean milk

Soak soybeans for at least 24 hours. Pour off the water, cover with boiling water and blend in a blender or processor – blend well, continuing for several minutes after the grounds appear to be fine.

Pour the liquid through a sieve, pressing well. Use at once, sweeten if required, or boil it for two minutes to 'pasteurise' it. Bottle and seal, and it should keep for a week or two in the fridge.

Sugars and sweeteners

Canary date palm

Sweet sap can be tapped from this tree at the flower stem in the same way that maple sugar is tapped.

Manna ash (*Fraxinus ornus*)

The manna ash is a broad crowned, attractive tree, up to 10 metres high with dense, white, fragrant flowers in spring. It likes full sun, tolerates cold to hot conditions and withstands drought. Propagate it from seed, suckers or by grafting.

If you tap the bark of the manna ash it will produce a sweet sticky sap that solidifies into a yellowish 'manna'. This can be boiled to a syrup and used for sweetening. However, the consumption of large quantities can lead to diarrhoea. Manna sap in hot milk was traditionally fed to children with mild constipation.

Sorghum

This is grown for sweet sorghum syrup or for stock food. Try Stock & Station agents for seed. Take care when growing sorghum: the plant is poisonous to stock. Grow it on less fertile soils for maximum sugar production. Slice the stalks, boil them in a very little water until it forms a syrup.

Sugar beet

When it is grown at all, sugar beet is mostly grown for stockfood in Australia. Ask at Stock & Station agents for sources of supply. Sugar beet should be grown like beetroot. To extract the sugar, you chop it and cook it in a little water until soggy, then strain it and reduce the liquid further until it forms a sweet syrup.

Sugar cane

As decorative as bamboo, sugar cane is normally subtropical, but it can be grown as far south as Sydney in any fairly frost-free area. The hotter the climate, and the more sun it gets, the more sugar it will produce. So don't be disappointed if you manage to grow it in a cool area but the juice isn't very sweet. On the other hand, a slight period of cool weather before harvesting will increase the sugar content of the cane – but you need hot weather first.

Sugar cane is propagated vegetatively, by planting sections of stalk, 35 to 40 cm long and carrying three to four buds. The canes will eventually grow up to 4 metres high and 5 cm in diameter. In cooler areas the canes will be much smaller, and may take two years or more to get to crop size. Sugar cane is very hungry, so feed and water it well if you want a high sugar content.

Sugar cane is usually harvested at ground level, and then the underground buds shoot again. Commercially, about three of these 'ratoon' crops are grown before the whole area is re-planted. For home growing you can just let the canes continue to re-grow.

Commercial sugar cane is crushed, and raw sugar is made from the extracted juice. For home sugar production, split the cane with an axe, chop it into pieces – as small as possible – and boil it in water until it forms a thick syrup. This will be brownish and very rich.

Sugar maple and silver birch

Sugar maples will do well in poor or rich soil, full sun or semi-shade. In cold areas the leaves turn deep yellow and red in autumn; in warmer areas they turn reddish and just fall off. Propagate sugar maples by seed.

Maple syrup comes form the sweet sap of the sugar maple tree, boiled down into syrup. Although the trees can be grown throughout cold to subtropical Australia, you will only get good quantities of maple syrup where there are cold nights and warm days to make the sap 'flow'. For small quantities, try driving a stake deep into the wood to release the sap in late winter, then boil this until it thickens. Silver birch trees also produce an excellent sweet sap, and can be tapped the same way as sugar maples.

Sugar wood (*Myoporum platycarpum*)

The Australian sugar wood is a small, dry country tree from eastern mainland Australia. It has slender drooping branches. A white manna is exuded from the trunk after wounds from insects or humans, and this sap eventually hardens into very sweet icicles.

Oils

Most people don't think it worthwhile growing your own oil crops, assuming that you can never harvest enough. This isn't true. Most oil bearing crops have an oil content of between 6 and 30 per cent. This means that for one bucketful of a crop you may get nearly one-third of a bucket of oil. A large patch of sunflowers or a couple of olive trees will yield enough for the needs of a moderate family.

Also, some of the oils listed below are specialist oils, and you don't need very much of them. And like all home-grown crops, home-grown and pressed oil is delicious – a wonder with salads and cooking. It is worthwhile producing even a little for special occasions.

Beechnut oil

Roast the nuts in a moderate oven until cooked through, grind them in a grinder or blender, place the pulp in a sieve and press out the oil. Store in sealed, sterilised jars. Beechnut oil is bitter if made from uncooked nuts.

Olive oil

Olive oil is one of the world's great oils. This is not just because it is one of the most delicious, but because olives are hardy, long-lived and tolerant of anything from drought to battles – they usually survive.

Olives are extraordinarily hardy, needing a hot, dry climate and tolerating minimum winter temperatures of as low as -12° C. They will grow on any rocky, dry hillside – but they grow faster on good, deep soil with adequate water. They will start to fruit in good conditions when they are from 4 to 6 years old, but they become really productive after about 50 years, and may still be bearing well after a thousand years!

Olives don't grow true to type from seed. They are best propagated from cuttings: take a 40 cm piece of hardwood, and stick it deep into the ground. If you do have fresh olive seeds though, try scattering them in the soil along a fence: in about ten years' time you may have a productive hedge.

There is no need to prune olives, but light pruning will ensure more new wood, and thus more fruit.

Extracting olive oil

Take ripe (black) or nearly ripe olives, including windfalls. If you are not bothered by birds, leave the olives on the tree until mid-winter to maximise oil production. If picked then, they should yield about 10 per cent of their weight in oil.

There is no need to pick olives individually – just shake the tree till the fruit falls onto a sheet or tarpaulin on the ground. The olives can either be used at once or left in the sun for a week or two to wilt.

Crushing

Olives and their stones must first be crushed. I have done this in a coffee grinder and meat mill, and once with a hammer, though that was messy. There are various small crushers on the market (for rock or bone rather than olive crushing), and if you were going to extract your own oil regularly it would be worth investing in one. When the olives and their stones are thoroughly crushed they are ready for pressing.

Pressing

Make a sack out of clean canvas. (For small amounts a stout pillowcase will do as well.) Half fill it with crushed olives. The oil must be pressed out of this.

Again, for large amounts it will be worthwhile fabricating a permanent screw press. But for a one-off go, cover a large flat rock or small firm table with a piece of plastic. The plastic should reach the ground. Prop the plastic up at the bottom so that it will catch the oil as it is pressed out.

Lay the sack of olive pulp on the plastic and cover it with a wide piece of solid board or metal. This should be pressed down to extract the oil and juice from the olives. Pressing down by hand won't be enough – try placing a very heavy stone on top and leaving it overnight. For a better result, make a lever out of a solid piece of wood, fastening it to the ground on one side and pressing it down across the sack.

As soon as the blackish juice stops coming through, take off the wooden top and pour boiling water onto the sack – just enough to make it wet. Now press again. Continue this process until the liquid that comes out is clear – in other words, mostly water. You will probably have to do this three or four times.

Siphon the black juice into jars and leave overnight. In the morning the oil will have floated to the top. Siphon it off as soon as possible; if it is left floating on the water for too long it will take up some of the bitter olive juice flavour.

Unless you like a very fruity, slightly bitter oil, it is best to strain the oil through some cotton wool wrapped in a clean tea-towel. Then pour the strained oil into clean jars, seal them, and store them away from heat and light. It should be delicious.

Quick-preserves olives

Take either green or black olives. Either take the stones out or prick them all over with a fork: as many holes as possible. Cover them with slightly salty water (even if you are on a no-salt diet, you must add salt at this stage), and quickly bring to the boil. Take them off the heat immediately. Leave them in the water overnight. The next morning drain off the water, cover with fresh non-salty water and leave for about two hours. Then change the water again. Repeat this for three days, changing the water at least four times a day.

Take the olives out of the water and wash them thoroughly under running water. Now place them in a marinade. I use half olive oil, half lemon juice, a lot of chopped garlic, and whatever herbs I fancy at the time – basil, tarragon and marjoram are all good. Leave the olives in the marinade in a cool place (but not the fridge) for 24 hours, and they are ready for eating.

Greek method of curing olives

Place your olives in a wicker basket or in an old fruit box with holes in the bottom. The holes will let the brine run out as the olives are cured. Cover the olives with a finger-thick layer of rock salt or, when there are a lot of olives, with alternate layers of olives and rock salt. Leave the olives in a cool place for 24 hours. Now put gloves on and mix the salt and olives thoroughly by hand. Do this once a day until the olives looked wrinkled. Add more salt if necessary. The whole process will take about six weeks and by then most of the bitterness from the olives will have been absorbed by the salt.

The olives can be stored in fresh rock salt or, better still, washed thoroughly to remove the salty taste and then stored in olive oil, with or without some chopped garlic, chilli, and oregano.

Peanut oil

Peanuts are a semi-tropical crop, but have been grown successfully as far south as Tasmania. They need well-drained, friable and very slightly acid soil.

Try buying raw peanuts and planting them about 9 cm apart as soon as frosts are over. The peanuts should grow into low bushes; the branches will sweep down to soil level; the 'nuts' will develop below these. Mulch well to increase your crop. Never use a peanut that looks mouldy.

To make peanut oil, grind the peanuts in a blender, mix with boiling water (don't boil the nuts) and leave overnight. Pour the oil off the top in the morning.

Safflower oil

Safflower is an annual herbaceous plant, once grown mostly as a dye. It is best sown in autumn so that it can branch and develop before spring-induced flowering. Plants sown early may have their flowers cut by frost, while later plantings will have lower yields. Safflower needs fairly dry conditions and should be sown in a well-prepared seedbed.

A substitute safflower oil can be made from the closely related saffron thistle, a common weed. Saffron thistle seeds yield about 16 per cent oil, about half the yield of safflower. For maximum oil yield, the seeds of both safflower and saffron thistle should be harvested when they are slightly unripe, then mashed and boiled in water. Leave overnight, and siphon off the layer of oil in the morning.

Sesame oil

This is grown both for the seeds themselves, and for the oil they contain. The seeds are high in calcium and protein, and the oil is low in cholesterol.

Sesame is a tall annual, with white trumpet-shaped flowers and seed capsules that burst when they are ripe, though non-shattering varieties have been developed for commercial use.

Sesame needs a frost-free, warm growing season. It takes four months and plenty of water for the seeds to ripen after flowering. You can try growing sesame from sesame seed: use brown, un-hulled seeds, not the white ones.

To make sesame oil, grind the seeds thoroughly in a blender. Empty the blender onto some clean cheesecloth suspended over a jar. Let the oil seep out with a little helpful pressing from you. Alternatively, bring the pulp to the boil and let it steep in water overnight. In the morning, you can siphon off the layer of oil from the top.

Tabini

You can eat sesame seeds like nuts. Or you can grind sesame seeds to make tahini. Add this to yoghurt, to lemon juice and garlic, or to ground chick peas or mashed eggplant for a rich dip. Sprinkle sesame seed on cakes and bread, or coat food in sesame seed instead of breadcrumbs before frying.

Sunflower oil

These are high-growing annuals with heavy seed heads and wide, yellow flowers. They will grow in almost any garden. The cheapest way to get seed is by buying a packet of parrot mix.

To harvest the seed, let the seed heads dry on the stalk till they shake out easily. Sunflower seeds can be hulled and eaten raw. They can also be fried in oil with garlic, or roasted and ground for coffee.

To make sunflower oil, pulverise the seeds or put them in a blender; then suspend them in cheesecloth over a jar and gently squeeze the pulp till all the oil is removed. For oil making, there is no need to hull the seeds. For a second pressing, pour boiling water over the pulped seeds, leave overnight, then strain off the oil.

Walnut oil

This can be made the same way as beechnut oil, though the nuts should not be roasted. Choose very ripe nuts, left to mature for at least a month after harvest. Walnut oil has been acclaimed as the best salad oil. It can also be poured over fresh, home-made pasta, with no other flavouring needed.

Chapter 3

Vegetables all year round

Most vegetable gardens are spring affairs. You dream about them in August and plant them out in spring – then they're weeds by Christmas.

A good garden should be able to feed you all year round. And I mean FEED you: not just a few carrots or green veg, but most of your fruit (melons, berries, apples, apricots, etc); protein from beans and peas and corn; and staples like potatoes.

All you need is good timing. Once you know when to plant, and how much, you're halfway there. Our vegie garden only takes about five minutes' work a week, not counting picking. You don't need to break your back or dedicate your weekends to growing enough vegetables to feed your family – just follow the points given in this chapter.

Good vegetable gardens are beautiful. It's a pleasure to wander round in them, admiring their fecundity. I can see our main vegetable garden from where I write. The tassels on the corn are turning gold; the beans are twisting through the trellises; there's enough celery to keep us through winter, and enough zucchini to feed a horde. The garden is fertilised with mulch from last year's weeds, and with the compost from the kitchen scraps ladled over it in spring. It is the basis of all our meals, year round: food that we know is fresh and unsprayed, with a flavour you never find in stale supermarket food. (Just taste a fresh onion or potato, and you realise what I mean.)

Most of all it is a healthy garden: there's no need for sprays, no need for any fungicides or pesticides. The soil – once so bad it wouldn't grow grass – is softer and richer every year, and the earthworms are so thick you can see them scuttling every time you pull up a carrot. Healthy soil means healthy vegetables. Don't worry about pests on your vegies – just concentrate on improving the soil, and you'll get the crops you need.

Rules for a healthy vegie garden

1 Don't dig your garden. If digging is your hobby, take up bowls instead – it's much better for the soil. Try the minimum-work gardens suggested in this chapter.
2 Grow flowers and vegetables together. Flowers attract predators which eat the pests. They also attract bees for pollination, and they help break up clumps of vegetables so that pests – which track their food either by shape or smell – will find it harder to find and attack your crops. Vegetables can be beautiful too. Try the bronze variety of ferny fennel for example, and consider the bright-yellow flowers of zucchinis as ornamentals, not as food. Potatoes were grown as ornamentals for their sweet, blue flowers well before the tubers became a popular food. Or you could try Swiss chard with multi-coloured stems, and admire the bright-red flowers of climbing beans, more vivid than sweet peas.
Don't plant straight, neat rows: they allow pests to start at one end and march down the row munching, like guests at a smorgasbord. Break up plantings so that there are no large groups of any one plant. Plant small plants near tall ones, shallow-rooters like lettuce near deep-rooters like carrots, and climbers next to long-stemmed corn or sunflowers.
3 Don't plant too early: spring growth is soft and sappy – just what pests like – and disease prone. Predators start to breed up some weeks after pests do. Wait until the ground warms up, until you can sit on the ground in comfort for a whole afternoon. Vegetables and flowers planted a little late will mature at the same time as earlier plantings anyway: cold, slow starts stunt them. Instead, start your seedlings in pots if you want big seedlings early.
4 Let the best vegetables go to seed. The flowers will attract the adult form of many predators, and the fresh, free seed this will give you the next year will be adapted to your garden.
5 Plant nitrogen fixers like beans, peas, sweet peas, broad beans, and peanuts: they add fertility to your garden as their residues break down.
6 Most importantly: don't exhaust yourself in spring, creating an enormous garden that you can't keep up with. Unless you like weeding, mulching, and thinning every week, you should use a minimum-work garden.

Minimum work, no-dig gardens

Weed-mat garden

Lay a weed mat over your mown lawn or weeds. Weigh it down. Cut out small holes. Plant seedlings in them. Water well. Feed once a fortnight with

capsicum

newspaper garden.

liquid manure, blood & bone or hen manure until the grass breaks down under the weed mat. This won't take long.

Seedlings in weed-mat gardens are slow to take off, but then do better than seedlings in comparable, dug beds next door.

Pull up the weed mat in autumn and plant thickly with onions and broad beans or peas. In spring, throw down the pea and broad bean debris and put down the weed mat again.

Above-ground garden

Heap up at least 10 cm of hay or dry lawn clippings. Then, either
• place small amounts of soil or compost on top, plant your seedlings, and water well, giving them liquid manure, hen manure or blood and bone until established; or
• part the hay, dig up a small patch with a tablespoon, and plant your seed or seedling in the tiny clear patch, surrounded by the hay.

The grass under the hay decays quickly with the fertiliser and watering; and the heat generated by the decay speeds up the plants growing on top of it.

Keep the plants well mulched with more hay or lawn clippings, and once they are established you should never have to weed, dig or fertilise again. Regular mulching will be all it needs.

Part the mulch temporarily for seeds like carrots. I rake the hay away, scatter the seeds, then rake the hay back again. No digging is needed.

Newspaper garden

This is for readers of the *Age* or *Sydney Morning Herald*, who need a truck to take away their weekend reading matter.

Mow your lawn. Plant your seedlings in the short grass. Surround them with newspaper. Weigh down the sheets with rocks or bits of wood. Now proceed as with the weed-mat garden. (But feed a little more, as the newspaper will temporarily lock up nitrogen whilst it decays.) Renew the newspaper as necessary, and use other mulch as well.

Making room

A self-sufficient vegetable plot need not take up most of the garden.
1 Plant close together. Most Australian gardeners plant too far apart. This is a relic from another culture: in English gardens you had to grab every available ray of sun. Our gardens need more shelter. Lots of leaf cover means the soil is insulated from heat and cold, and the plants get more protection against frost. If one plant dwarfs another, the small one will grow to size after you've picked its neighbour.
2 Don't plant in neat rows, with neat paths in between. This is bad for the soil, and good for pests, which can see what they're eating that way. Plant everything together, and tread warily in between.

3 Grow upwards: have as many trellises as you can manage. Six metres of climbing beans crops as much as six metres on the ground. We have climbing tomatoes, beans, peas, sweet peas, cucumbers, berries, melons, and butternut pumpkins (most other pumpkins tend to be too heavy). If you can find a climbing variety of a plant, use it in preference to a dwarf one.

4 Forget about neat crop rotation. As long as you plant lots of nitrogen fixers like beans, peas, sweet peas, broad beans, lupins, etc, the whole garden will get the benefit as they decay back into the soil. And anyway, your garden should be so varied that it is unlikely to suffer the consequences that come with planting the same crop year after year.

Instead, whenever you pull something out, put something back in its place. Follow a giant cauliflower with a clump of twenty bean seeds; follow a patch of lettuces with carrot seed; put corn seedlings in as you pull out celery. If you've nothing ready to plant, put in quick-growing radish seeds – then pull them up for mulch. This will not only save space, it will stop the bare soil from being damaged by wind and water, and it will stop weeds, which love to colonise bare soil.

So, always, *always*, ALWAYS: plant as soon as you harvest!

Planting times for year-round vegetables

There are four main planting times if you want enough vegetables to see you through the year. About half your vegetable crop can be planted in spring and can then be harvested the next spring.

Spring

Plant enough of the 'all year' vegetables to see you through the year: all year lettuce (you pick a leaf as you need it); celery, carrots, beetroot (eat the leaves too), parsnips, parsley, leeks (eat the tiny ones too and plant them thickly), spring onions (eat the greens), garlic (just eat the tops chopped in salads or soup), broccoli (as long as you pick it every day, or it toughens), silverbeet, collards (like a non-hearting cabbage: hardy and good), and foliage turnips (just eat the tops). These plants can also be sown throughout summer if space is scarce.

Plant frost-sensitive crops like corn, tomatoes, potatoes, melons, eggplant, cucumber, capsicum, beans, zucchini, radish, pumpkins, and chilli.

Then, until January, just plant successions of corn, beans, lettuce, radish – or any of the above crops you've forgotten to put in, or now have room for.

January

Plant the main winter, autumn and spring crops of cabbage, brussels sprouts, cauliflowers, broccoli, swedes, turnips, foliage turnips, etc.

Plant more tomatoes, zucchini and cucumber, so you have vigorous plants that will crop well as the weather cools down or in case earlier plantings get mildewed.

Plant garlic and more potatoes.

Then, until winter – for cropping next spring – plant more cabbage, brussels sprouts, broccoli, red cabbage, and winter lettuce.

Autumn

As the ground cools down, plant peas, broad beans, early onions and late brassicas, and English spinach and winter lettuces for spring eating.

Winter

Plant your main onion crop.

As well as this:

• plant something every week, and
• plant whenever you take something out.

Watering

Plants need water to carry their nutrients and to soften the soil. Water when the soil is dry just below the surface or under the mulch. Mulched plants need less water; deep rooted perennials also need less water and their leaves will shade the annuals. Mulch with anything – even rocks of newspaper, to cool the soil and keep in moisture; install a drip irrigation system if you have the time and money. (If you install it yourself a drip system can actually be cheaper than the equivalent length of hose.)

In hot weather, if you are going to be away for a few days, try upending a bottle of water with a small hole pierced in the lid, next to fragile plants or seedlings. Moisture will slowly trickle out of the hole. You can do the same with a bucket of water, preferably with a lid and, again, with a small hole in the bottom.

Fertilising

Feed your flowers and vegies with mulch: dry lawn clippings, old leaves, straw, hay, dry manure. Use blood & bone, liquid manure, hen manure, etc. only in an emergency, or if the mulch doesn't contain many nutrients. With mulches like comfrey, lucerne hay, seaweed, old lawn clippings and compost you won't need much else. Try and vary their diet though, and do try to give some compost at least every other year.

It is almost impossible to give vegies and flowers too much mulch; just make sure the leaves are not covered by it.

Extras

For plants that need more feeding, or whilst you are waiting for your mulch to break down, try: blood & bone, pelletized or old hen manure, or liquid manure, either home-made or commercial.

Home-made liquid manure

Take a bucket or drum with a lid. Fill it with as many of the following as you can: weeds, manure, human urine, hay, seaweed, fresh lawn clippings, comfrey, nettles, chamomile, and yarrow. Cover this with water, put the lid on, and leave a few days. Dilute to a pale-yellow colour or it may be too strong. Then dip out the liquid for fertilizer, as needed.

Weeding

Annual weeds can just be cut or the tops pulled off. Perennial weeds can be dug out (often difficult); mulched over (try a thick paper mulch with a rock on top); covered with clear plastic; or just accepted as a source of fertilizer and mulch. But cut them often, in that case, before they seed.

There is no place for grass in a flower or vegetable garden: grass slows the growth of other plants, not just by competing for nutrients and water, but by releasing growth inhibitors. Keep grass out with a grass barrier (just use a piece of metal bent over at the top and pushed into the soil – this also keeps out snails), or with a thick line of deep-rooted plants like comfrey. We grow comfrey round our garden: it keeps out both couch and kikuyu. Comfrey dies down in winter in the frost, but the grass stops growing then too, and in spring comfrey starts growing before the grasses do.

Other plants can also be used as grass barriers, though I've found comfrey the best. Try a thick mat of marjoram (it will need two years' growth before it keeps out grass), thickly-planted chicory, dwarf canna lilies, or catnip; or you could even try a three-deep, closely planted row of radishes, while waiting for slower growing plants to take off.

Pest control

Don't worry about pests and diseases – just grow more plants, to compensate. The more productive and varied a garden is, the healthier it tends to be anyway. After all, you're there more often, picking its produce, and thus you tend to notice weeds and pests in time to nip them in the bud. As a last resort you could try glue spray: mix one cup of flour with one cup of boiling water, then add cold water till you can spray it. Glued-up pests stop eating, and are easy prey for birds and other predators which gobble them up.

If you want to kill your garden pests neatly, instead of suffocating them, use a pyrethrum spray.

Speeding up your crops

- Keep them well-fed and watered.
- Use a plant tonic made by soaking nettles, seaweed and chamomile in water for a week, then spraying the strained liquid over the plants. This should give them an added fertilizer boost and increase their resistance to heat stress.
- A heat-absorbing, dark mulch around plants will speed up their growth, as will a reflective aluminium mulch.
- Dandelions grown around plants release ethylene that helps ripening. Couch grass is said to do the same. But the root exudations of couch grass also inhibit the growth of other plants. So, with couch grass, what you gain on the swings you'll more than lose on the roundabouts.
- Weeding isn't a high priority. Contrary to popular belief, by the time your plants are one-third grown, *new* weeds won't impede their growth much: they should be able to outcompete them easily. In addition, the added leaf cover of weeds with their insulating warmth may actually speed up other plants' maturing. This is especially true for dandelion which produces ethylene, a natural ripener. Try growing dandelions among marginal crops like okra or eggplant or early tomatoes which you want to mature a little faster. Crops under apple trees are also reputed to come to maturity faster, though competition for moisture and light may counter this.

The easiest vegetables

The easiest veg to grow is probably silverbeet: plant it in spring, then eat it all year. It is closely followed by pumpkin, tomato, lettuce, spring onion and choko. If you're just beginning a vegetable garden I would plant these first, and extend your range as you get used to vegetable gardening.

The only really difficult vegetables to grow are slow starters like carrots and onions: they can be taken over by weeds before they've grown much. Otherwise, if your soil is good – or you've covered your seedlings with a good mulch – your vegetables should mostly grow themselves. After all, that's what plants have been doing for thousands of years without human help. All you have to do is supply a good beginning: good soil or good mulch, and water when your plants need it.

The perennial vegetable garden

The perennial vegetable garden should be the basis of your vegetable eating: vegies that you plant once, feed and water – and keep picking, year after year.

Perhaps one-third of our vegetable consumption at home is perennial. It means less work and less soil disturbance, whilst the plants become more frost and drought hardy as their roots grow bigger every year.

Artichokes These are a tough form of thistle. Sow artichoke seed in spring, or plant the roots in winter.

Eat the young flower heads in spring. After the first big heads have formed, little ones follow. Eat them all. The plants multiply every year. The more you feed and water them, the more you get; but they'll crop even under extreme neglect.

Asparagus This is the first spring crop: fat, tender spears that will keep shooting for months. We eat asparagus twice a day from September to December. Modern varieties crop in two years. Don't be put off by its reputation as hard to grow – asparagus just needs feeding. Ours has survived scratching lyrebirds, drought, fire and flooding; but with a bit of mulch it's soon as good as new.

Plant the crowns in winter or the seed in spring. Don't bother with complicated techniques. I just slice off the grass and lay ours on the ground, and cover them with mulch or compost. I add more compost or mulch every winter. And that's it.

Pick your asparagus as the new shoots come up in spring. Only pick ones that are as thick as your finger. If they are smaller, the plant needs more food or is too young to harvest. Leave it till next year.

You can usually pick your asparagus for three months of the year – longer if you feed and water it well.

Beans, perennial These are also called five or seven-year beans, or penny beans. They are a climbing bean with bright red flowers. They don't set fruit in mid-summer, but give a good spring and autumn crop, and just keep coming up every year. The roots get bigger with every season. Even when they don't bear fruit they look tall and bright and wonderful.

Sow the seed in spring. Pick the beans young as they tend to get tough later. Leave the surplus on the vine to dry. They make lovely dried beans for winter eating: pink-and-black spotted and very sweet.

Chicory Eat the leaves. Dig up the root in autumn and eat it like parsnip.

Chives These clumps are a reliable stand-by for greens or onion flavour. We add them to almost anything from omelettes to salads and stews, or scattered on meat, potatoes or carrots.

Sow seed in spring or summer, or divide a clump. They die down in winter, though Siberian chives are hardier if you can get hold of them.

Chokos These are not for cold areas. We go down to minus 5° C here in winter, and our bush is in a sheltered spot: I think that is about the coldest a choko can stand. One vine yields enough to keep a family in chokos all year. If you could bear to eat so many chokos, that is.

Plant a shooting choko in spring; feed and water it well. It will die down during frost; mulch the roots well if the ground freezes. In cool areas you may not get much of a crop until late autumn, but small chokos are sweeter than big ones.

Corn salad

Also called lamb's lettuce, this is a perennial green, but is often grown as an annual because the leaves turn bitter in hot weather. Make sure you only pick new leaves in the heat. Though corn salad is hardy and drought tolerant, the leaves are more succulent if the plant is well treated.

Sow the seed in spring; feed and water well.

Dandelions

The improved culinary varieties are much larger leafed than the wild weed. Eat the leaves in spring, before they get bitter in the heat, or cover the plant with a box for a week to 'blanch' the leaves to make them sweeter in mid-summer. The roots are also good, like a sweet parsnip.

Sow the seed in spring and summer.

Egyptian mint

This is a large-leafed, mild mint. Good in salads, it can even be steamed as a vegetable. New potatoes or fish steamed in Egyptian mint are wonderful.

Sow the seed in spring, or transplant runners.

Fennel

This can become a weed. Eat the bulbs stewed or grated raw, or the tops wrapped round fish, or finely chopped in salads or stews.

Sow the seed at any warm time of the year. Fennel dies down in the frost but comes back in spring, with a thousand small plants round it.

French sorrel

This loves acid soils. It is slightly bitter, but good in soups and in a sauce to accompany fish. A little is good in a salad.

Garlic

Plant the cloves in February for the best bulbs, or at any warm time of the year. Pull up the new bulb when the tops die off or, like us, just leave them in the ground and use the green tops as needed, and the mass of thin green stems as 'garlic leeks'. The clumps get bigger every year, and the young stems and new tops are delicious.

Garlic chives

These are flat, broad chives with a pronounced garlic flavour. *See* chives.

Ginger

Ginger is for warm areas only. Grow it like sweet potatoes, Japanese hornwort and Jerusalem artichokes.

Good King Henry

This is a tall plant – its leaves are added to salads when young, and should be cooked when old. They are as bland as lettuce but a bit tougher.

Japanese hornwort

This is grown for its leaves, which can be used like spinach. The leaves are a bit too aromatic for tastes attuned to the blandness of silverbeet, for example. But the more you feed and water hornwort, the blander it gets.

Sow the seed in spring. It will tolerate mild frost.

Jerusalem artichokes

These are a root vegetable, knobbly but good. They do produce wind, however, so eat them with friends or alone. Plant a few artichokes in late winter or spring – grub them up from mid-summer onwards, as needed, or dig them out when the tops die down. Once you've got them, though, you'll always have them – they are very difficult to get rid of.

Kumeras

These are really an annual, but they will come up every year from bits left the previous year. Buy the tubers from a good greengrocer. They are 'New Zealand sweet potato' (really a form of oxalis), and they tolerate frost. Keep them weed-free.

Leaves   Some leaves are edible: try young lemon leaves in salads, or instead of vanilla flavouring in a custard; dry and crumble avocado leaves for an avocado flavour in stuffings. Young vine leaves can be eaten like lettuce – or stuff and stew them as in stuffed cabbage. Try a few nasturtium leaves in salad sandwiches to give them bite, or stuffed and stewed like cabbage leaves. Young hop or choko shoots are also good, though the older leaves are bitter.

Lemon or lime balm   This is a fragrant herb. Eat the young leaves like lettuce or in sandwiches.

Sow the seed at any warm time of the year. It spreads readily, and likes lots of moisture. The more you water and feed it, the more tender and mild the leaves will be.

Lovage   Use the leaves like celery and the root, which tastes like celery too, like sweet potato. (Once you eat the root though, you've lost your plant, of course.)

Sow the seed at any time of year. Lovage is very hardy.

New Zealand spinach   This is an improved weed. It runs along the ground with pointed leaves, and loves moist, fertile ground. It crops as well in cold as in hot climates. It's a bit fleshier than ordinary spinach, but still good.

Rhubarb   Some rhubarbs are small and red, some are fat and green; some produce through winter, but most die down. All are hardy, once established. The more you feed and mulch them the more you'll get.

Rocket   This is a peppery salad green. It re-seeds itself after flowering, and it spreads. It is also very hardy.

Sorrel   Once you have sorrel you'll always have it. It is perennial, but it seeds and spreads. A bit bitter, it makes a good soup, sauce for fish, or addition to salads.

Sweet potato   This is for frost-free or mild frost areas only. Plant a sprouting sweet potato in spring. Dig up the roots as you need them and let the rest continue to grow. In cold areas try growing sweet potato as an annual – though you will only get a small crop in short summers. If you have mild frosts, mulch the ground well so the roots don't freeze.

Tamarillo   Its oval red, yellow or orange fruit hangs from a tall shrub or small tree, and is both sweet and acid, like tomatoes. Thus, they are also known as tree tomatoes. You can eat them in fruit salads, or in salads like tomatoes, but they can't be added to soups or stews.

Tamarillo grows quickly from seed, and fruits within a year, or you can propagate it from a cutting in late winter.

Tamarillo tolerates about three degrees of frost. Even if all its leaves disappear, they'll come back in spring and it will bear a late autumn crop. In mild areas tamarillo crops all year round.

Making annual vegetables perennial

- Pick lettuce leaf by leaf. Choose cos or mignonette, not iceberg. Pick out the seed stalk as it appears. The leaves will get smaller and, unless you feed it as often as you pick it, the leaves will gradually get bitter.
- Pick broccoli every day, and feed it. Don't let it flower. I once kept one for

three years, then went on holiday. When I got back it had become inedible.

- Pick silverbeet every day and pick out the seed head stalks as they appear: they'll be tall and thick. It will keep branching with smaller and more numerous leaves.
- Pick out the tops of celery. It will branch and become thinner. But if you continue to feed and water it, it will stay tender at least until your next crop is ready.
- Graft tomatoes onto a long-lived, frost-hardy native solanum, like kangaroo berry.
- Don't pull up all your potatoes. Burrow underneath (a potato bandicoot) and just take what you need. The other potatoes will re-grow. You can do the same with kumeras (in cool areas) and sweet potato (in warm areas), or with arrowroot (in hot to cool, temperate areas).
- Don't pull up garlic, but eat the tops instead.
- When you pick a cauliflower, don't pull out the stalk. It will produce more small heads. Pick these whilst they are firm, or they get tough, especially in hot weather. They may turn yellow or purple in summer. Don't worry about that though.
- Don't pull out spring onion bulbs. Mine have been in for six years. We just eat the tops and they keep multiplying.

Growing the basics all year round

I'm not a peasant. Peasants eat what's in season. I grew up expecting to eat onions whenever I wanted them, lettuce salad all year round, and tomato soup in winter.

This takes a bit of fiddling. You can either grow enough to store or freeze, or try some of the following methods.

A year of carrots

I plant all our carrots in spring. If space is tight, you can keep planting carrot seed till late summer. I like to grow several varieties, as my tastes vary from year to year. I suppose that means not one carrot variety is really outstanding, but also that variety is fun.

Tiny carrots will be ready for thinning after about two months. Eat them small and sweet and leave room for the others to expand. Carrots get sweeter through winter. In early spring, mulch the ground well around your carrots to keep it cold, so your carrots don't go to seed until the next lot are ready for thinning.

Deeply dug or soft soil gives long straight roots. Our carrots wriggle because I don't dig. But they are still thick and sweet.

Varieties (among many others)

Round French
Small round carrots, good for growing in boxes or on stony soil, or if you want a quick crop in spring or before winter.

Western red
One of the mammoths, dark and sweet and big.

Topweight
Ditto.

Amsterdam forcing
A quick-growing 'baby' carrot.

A year of greens

In spring we gorge on asparagus and artichokes and broad beans; in autumn and early summer it's peas; in summer we dine on at least four different sorts of beans; in winter there's brussels sprouts and broccoli and true English spinach. We eat lettuce and cabbage, leeks and silverbeet, turnip tops and celery all year round.

I plant enough silverbeet and celery and leeks in spring to last all year. All like lots of food and water, as does any crop that's picked a lot. Never pick the whole silverbeet or celery plant: just leaf by leaf or stalk by stalk. If you have plenty of silverbeet and celery you've got greens whenever you need them. If you have masses of leeks you've got luxury.

I plant a new lot of beans whenever the last lot flowers; and I plant peas in spring and from January to March, so they mature in cold weather. In January I also plant enough broccoli and other brassicas to see us through the winter.

A year of tomatoes

Our worst frost was minus 8°C this year (usually it only goes down to minus 5), but I was still able to pick two large tomatoes a week from an outside bush, and a cupful of cherry tomatoes. Still, it wasn't worth it. The tomatoes were a nice red colour but tasteless, almost bitter. I should have grated beetroot into our salads for colour instead, and relied on bottled or dried tomatoes for cooking.

How did I do it though? I built a walled garden (or rather Bryan did): stone terraces facing the morning sun with heat absorbing paving stones below and the warmth of the house nearby reflecting heat too. The top terraces were the warmest. I crowded the tomato plants with cauliflowers to insulate them, and I kept the soil below covered in calendulas which trap heat too. The tomato plants were still growing in spring.

Another tomato that survived the winter was a climbing yellow tomato, wandering up and around an old spreading tamarillo. The tamarillo insulated it, at least until it got frosted off too (it re-grew). But the yellow tomatoes had no more flavour than the others.

I find cherry tomatoes the most frost resistant, especially if buried in the rest of the garden's jungle. Grafted tomatoes also tolerate cold, and may sprout again the next year, except in very cold areas. Tomatoes planted in late summer survive early frost better than the tired old ones from spring.

You can also graft your own tomatoes onto native frost-resistant stock like kangaroo berry. The trouble is that kangaroo berry isn't a prolific grower, so you'll get very few tomatoes, whether it's summer or winter. But if you are keen on winter tomatoes you could try it – or build a glasshouse instead.

A simpler solution is to dig up your tomatoes in autumn and pot them; or to grow new ones in pots, planted in late summer so they are in full vigour for winter. Keep them indoors at night, and put them out in the sun during the day. They will be sweeter than my outdoor winter tomatoes, but still not as sweet as tomatoes which get the summer sun.

Ripening green tomatoes

If your bush is too big to dig up and pot, pull it up by the roots and leave it in the shed. The tomatoes on it will keep ripening as their stems keep feeding them for some time.

Alternatively, just spread the tomatoes on newspaper in a warm room. They'll gradually ripen over the next three months. Inspect them every few days and toss out bad ones. When they are ripe, they won't be as sweet as the ones you picked at the height of summer, but will still have more flavour than shop-bought tomatoes.

A year of lettuce

During summer I plant a punnet of lettuce – about twelve plants – every week. Any we don't eat get thrown around the garden as mulch: nothing is wasted in the self-sufficient garden. I like the small, sweet mignonette that can be grown all year round. But there are literally dozens of other varieties to choose from: one of the advantages of growing your own is the chance to gourmandise. There are now punnets available that contain several sorts of lettuce, all maturing at different times: excellent for people who only need a couple at weekends.

I plant masses of lettuce in autumn, enough to see us through the winter. Although mignonette and other winter lettuce are frost resistant, they don't grow much in cold weather. As soon as the ground warms up I put in more: small sweet mignonettes are ready to eat about eight weeks after planting, but individual leaves can be pulled off after one month.

Consider growing the following varieties:
- Mignonette (red or green) all year round.
- Red or green cos lettuce: pull a leaf as you need them – they're great if you only want a few lettuce leaves at a time.
- Oak leaf lettuce (red or green) for a frilly extravaganza.
- If you like old-fashioned, crisp-headed lettuces, there are many varieties like the common summer iceberg, heat-resistant Narromar, or winter's green velvet.

How to grow lettuce

Lettuce needs lots of water and lots of food or you'll get bitter lettuce. This is caused by any setback to their growth: usually moisture stress, but sometimes lack of fertiliser. Keep lettuce growing strongly if you want them to be sweet: water every day, mulch them to even out fluctuations in soil temperature, to control weeds and to keep the soil fertile and humus-rich.

Too much water in hot weather can make some types of lettuce puffy instead of firm-hearted. I like to grow summer lettuce under the corn or in the shade of the beans. If your lettuces fail to heart it's probably because they've had too much nitrogen and water, especially during hot weather. Stick to organic fertilisers, steadily releasing nutrients from organic matter, manures, blood & bone or, if necessary, a liquid manure.

If you have slimy lettuce, try mulching heavily and watering less (especially overhead watering), and make sure your lettuce aren't grown in the same spot year after year. To keep down fungal and bacterial conditions, allow at least two other crops to grow before you re-plant with lettuce. Don't plant lettuce near dandelions, chicory or endive: they share the same range of pests and diseases.

A year of onions

Onion planting is simple. Even though different varieties have different optimum times for planting, if you follow the general rules you'll get a good crop.

Basically, cold weather means large bulbs, and warm weather means green tops. So, plant spring onions in spring (or at any other time of the year when the soil is warm enough for them to germinate), and other onions from autumn through winter. An exception are the flat white onions that don't keep well. Plant these in early autumn so they'll have a good amount of leaf growth before winter. This will give you crisp, fresh, sweet onions in spring and throughout summer. The other main crop onions will mature from mid-summer through to autumn. I've found that sweet, red salad onions can be planted at any time, though late winter gives the biggest bulbs.

Be adventurous with your onions. Fresh onions don't taste at all like shop-bought ones. Home-grown onions have flavour as well as acidity.

Plant lots of varieties. They all vary wonderfully in taste as well as in their keeping ability. A wide range of onions will give you fresh ones to harvest most of the year, as well as a good number for storage. Only a few of the many varieties available are given here.

Spring onions
Also called salad onions or white bunching onions, these can be quite bulbous at the bottom, or simply be straight green leaves, or in between, depending on the variety. You can harvest them indefinitely once they are planted, as long as you don't take too many stems at once. Some of our clumps have been growing for over a decade.

Pickling onions
There are many varieties. Plant them from May to August for harvesting from December to March.

Flat white onion
This is like the white Spanish onion. Plant them from May to June for harvesting from spring to mid-summer.

Galadan brown onion
This is a mild onion, not for storage. Plant it in late autumn, and harvest from spring to mid-summer.

Tropic gold
This is an onion for hot climates. Plant it in autumn for a spring harvest.

Red odourless
Plant it in autumn for a spring to mid-summer harvest.

Pukehoe
This is my favourite storing onion. Planted in mid-winter it gives a late summer harvest.

How to grow onions
Onions grow slowly. Weeds grow fast. Make sure your onions are weed free from the beginning. To germinate any weed seeds, cover your soil with clear plastic for a month before planting, or plant the onions where the weed mat has been in summer for other crops.

Don't mulch too close to your onions, as the necks can rot. Don't use fresh manure or blood & bone either, or you may attract bulb boring pests.

A year of corn

Corn is one of the world's great staples: not just for eating fresh, but for making porridge, cornbread and polenta, for adding to soups and stews, and for feeding to stock.

I have managed to grow corn here all year round, with the temperature descending to minus 5° C one winter. I don't know if it was worth the trouble. After all, corn for cooking and animals is easily stored. (See Chapter 8). But the fresh cobs of corn were a treat in late winter and spring. Even if they were fairly tasteless by home-grown corn-on-the-cob standards, they were still better than frozen corn.

Plant your main lot of corn in spring. I find the first lot matures unevenly, so your crop will be staggered over about a month. Plant the next lot about six weeks later, then plant at three weekly intervals. An alternative is to plant both early, mid-season, and late maturing varieties of corn at the same time, and then some more around Christmas.

If you want to 'overwinter' corn, plant more in late summer, about a month before the first frost. As soon as the soil starts to cool down, and trees begin to show their colours, mulch the corn heavily (*very* heavily), right up to the tips of the green leaves.

Mulch attracts frost and the leaves above it will tend to freeze. With this method there are no leaves above the mulch – or almost none. Push the mulch down on sunny days, and fluff it right up at night. The trapped air will insulate the plants and the soil, and stop both from freezing.

An alternative is to throw old tyres over each corn plant, or to plant your corn in the tyres to begin with: about two plants per tyre. Keep piling on the tyres as they grow; and keep throwing in mulch as you put on the tyres. Don't cover the plant entirely, and make sure that the mulch is well below the level of the tyre: the black will absorb warmth and the tyres will insulate the plants. I find that a quick-growing crop of radish, thrown around the corn on a bit of soil on top of the mulch, also reduces frost damage.

The corn will mature very slowly, and won't be very sweet. But for corn addicts, year-round fresh corn is possible in this way, even in frost areas.

Summer corn

I plant a lot of corn in early spring: usually two varieties that mature at different times. I find this 'lump sowing' provides all the corn we need until late January: thickly planted corn matures at different times. I then plant more corn just before Christmas, and again in late January. If you want to carefully stagger your corn, plant it every two weeks – or whenever you plant more beans, i.e. when the last lot of beans are flowering.

A year of potatoes

We had massive frosts last year: down to minus 8° C, which is unusual for our valley. But the potatoes still kept growing. Not the ones in the soil, of course; they'd died off by May. These ones were planted in tyres, under the shelter of an avocado tree. I piled up tyres two deep; threw a potato onto the grass; threw down some weeds, and left them. They grew by themselves as the weeds gradually rotted into soil and the grass below the potato died. I kept throwing in more weeds to keep them mulched almost to the top of the plant.

The 'winter spuds' were only small: bantam egg size. But they were welcome as the potatoes in the cupboards were beginning to sprout, and they kept us going till the spring crop was ready to bandicoot.

I grow potatoes in tyres in early spring and autumn. The rest of the time they grow faster in the ground. Or rather, I toss them on the ground and cover them with mulch. The more you mulch potatoes, or hill the soil around them, the more spuds you get. Potatoes form on potato branches: if you cover the branches you get more spuds.

Plant your first potatoes about six weeks before the last frost date; here (the Araluen Valley, NSW), that is the beginning of August. The spuds will take about six weeks to sprout and leaf, and are fairly invulnerable to cold until then – unless the ground freezes, in which case they'll rot.

Potatoes in a pile of weeds

This year we pruned our kiwi fruit, which left a great heap of jungley rubbish. I threw in a few potatoes and covered the lot with straw. Four months later we had a heap of potatoes. If we throw our prunings onto this heap every year, and the potatoes don't get infected by any aphid-borne disease, we'll keep getting potatoes from our pile of weeds indefinitely.

Bandicooting potatoes

Potatoes should be harvested when the tops die down. The skins are toughest then, and the spuds will store well. Young spuds don't store. But you can pick potatoes before the tops die down by wriggling your hand under the mulch or soil and carefully pulling out the small ones. Disturb the roots as little as possible, so they go on producing more spuds.

I don't dig up all our spuds. I always leave a few – and just bandicoot when I need them.

A year of garlic

Garlic gives the fattest bulbs when planted about February, so the bulbs mature in cool weather. But you'll get garlic if you plant a clove at any warm time of the year. Harvest for storage when the tops begin to yellow; hang the bulbs by their stalks in a dry place (or plait the stalks in traditional fashion and hang them in the kitchen.

Our garlic is perennial now. I rarely pull up a bulb. I use the green tops instead, chopping them into stews and salads. They are strongly garlic-flavoured. (I also use garlic chives.) Sometimes, in winter, I pull up a whole garlic plant, and use it like a leek. They are delicately garlicky, and incredibly delicious – especially stewed in olive oil with a few sun-dried tomatoes.

Using waste vegetable bits

Parts of vegetables can be 'harvested' even if they aren't really mature. Try parsnip tops. Use them like celery in stews and soup or finely grated in salads. Beetroot tops can substitute for silverbeet, as can turnip tops. When these are young and tender they are also excellent raw. Try young turnip tops grated up in mashed potatoes. You should try eating garlic tops (raw or cooked) instead of the bulbs, or the leafy tips of broad beans, the leaves of broccoli or brussels sprouts, or zucchini or pumpkin flowers. The latter are wonderful: stuff them with leftover fried rice and stew them in stock, or dip them – stuffed or plain – in egg, then breadcrumbs, and deep-fry them. Serve them with lemon juice or hollandaise sauce.

You can tell the male flowers – most of which are expendable – from the female ones by looking for the swelling at the base of the flower.

Using immature vegetables

Unmatured corn cobs can be kept on the stalk by bending the stalk over them, to shelter them from frost and rain so they won't rot before they mature. They will continue to mature slowly this way until the talks are almost brittle. Young corn, Chinese style, is delicious. Whenever you pull out a corn stalk, run your fingers down the leaves to make sure an immature cob isn't forming. If it is – pluck, stir-fry and enjoy!

Tiny cucumbers – as small as they come – are even better than the big ones, either raw or cooked. A Chinese friend introduced me to them and they have become my favourite vegetable. Try frying thin slices with a little ginger and garlic for 10 seconds on as high a heat as you can get.

Pumpkins can be eaten as soon as they form behind the flower – they'll be just like small squash, which is, in fact, what they are. They won't taste as sweet as mature pumpkin – more mellow and nutty, like zucchini.

Try picking small watermelons before they turn pink inside. Use a sweet, well-spiced marinade. It's not that the melon will taste of much – the only taste will be of the pickling solution – but the texture can be excellent.

Carrot, beetroot, parsnip, turnip and the like can all be picked and eaten as soon as you can be bothered with them. The smaller the sweeter. But all these vegetables should continue to mature through winter as long as the ground doesn't freeze – especially under a thick bed of mulch.

Cook lettuce that hasn't hearted – in stock, to eat by itself and for lettuce soup, or wrap it round rice for stuffed 'cabbage'.

Green tomatoes can be pickled, or you can make green tomato chutney or jam with them.

How much to plant

This is a hard one. Family tastes vary. If you don't like cabbage there's no sense in planting any – but then you'll have to make up for that by growing more of something else.

I know what I grow for the three of us – two adults who eat three meals a day here, one kid with a large appetite who is at school for most of the day, and the odd horde of visitors, who also mostly have large appetites (or they do by the time they've wandered up the creek and back, and picked some oranges). But his won't be the same for a couple who are at work all week, or a family with four teenage kids.

We also have a large perennial garden with masses of asparagus, artichokes, tamarillos, etc. This reduces our needs from the annual garden.

So, work out your own needs. Work out, for example, how many cabbages you eat a week, and multiply by 52. I usually plant something like the following quantities.

Beans	One packet in spring, followed by another packet when the last lot flowers through summer. We usually grow several sorts. Grow more, of course, if you want them dried.
Beetroot	Two punnets: we're not beetroot eaters.
Broad beans	About two square metres in May, but plant more if you want them dried. Broad beans crop at the same time as artichokes and asparagus – and I like asparagus more than broad beans.
Broccoli	Twenty-four plants in mid-summer.
Brussels sprouts	Twelve plants in mid-summer.
Cabbage	About 50 small cabbages in late summer, and a dozen cabbages and red cabbage in spring for coleslaw.
Capsicum	One dozen in spring.
Carrots	One square metre of carrots per month (we eat a lot of carrots though – so does the resident wombat). I plant these all in spring. If you don't eat many carrots one square metre may do for a year.
Cauliflower	Thirty in late summer.
Celery	One dozen plants are enough if they are very well fed. You need two dozen if you want to eat a lot in salads.
Chilli	A dozen plants, once a decade.
Corn	About 50 plants in spring, then more throughout the summer.
Cucumber	One dozen vines planted in spring, and another dozen in January. (But note that Edward and I adore cucumbers; two vines may be enough for other people.)
Eggplant	One bush because I'm the only one who eats it – if the others did we'd have to grow about a dozen.
Leeks	About 100: I love leeks and use them instead of onions in winter stews.
Lettuce	Twelve a week for most of the year except mid-winter. Plant about 30 in late summer for winter lettuce.
Melons	As many as we can – you can't have too many watermelons and rockmelons!
Onions	About 400 seedlings with six bunches of perennial spring onions and lots of chives and shallots.
Parsley	Three dozen plants, kept well fed.
Parsnips	None, as ours are self-seeding. We eat about one square metre of them per year. But as parsnip only germinate when they are fresh, and as most seed is stale, you may have to sow a lot the first time in order to get a few. Then, let one go to seed and you'll have more than you need thereafter.
Peas	Three packets in autumn, and three in spring; but here the wombat eats most of them!
Potatoes	We eat about 200 kilos a year (Bryan is a potato eater). Most of these come from 'perennial' spuds – ones that come up every year. You probably need to plant a large sack of seed potatoes for a year's supply – or even two if you eat a lot of them. Once you grow your own you'll probably eat more potatoes than you used to: fresh potatoes are nothing like stale ones from the shops.

Pumpkin	A dozen vines, including at least two of bush pumpkins.
Radish	Normally one packet each of about six varieties, sown throughout the year – though now ours seed themselves so I rarely have to plant any.
Silverbeet	Twenty-four plants.
Tomatoes	Three grafted tomatoes, a dozen ordinary plants, one cherry tomato, one egg tomato, and one climbing yellow tomato. This gives us enough to preserve too.
Zucchini	Two plants in spring, and two in mid-summer.

Then there are the vegies I grow to add fun to our garden and our diet: spaghetti squash, corn salad, cress, endives, mustard greens, rosellas, English spinach, edible chrysanthemum, Chinese bitter gourd, chicory, borecole or curly kale, okra, fennel, Chinese cabbage, collards, turnips, foliage turnips (we grow these most years), and many others.

I don't grow all of these every year: some are just ignored – we never did get round to more than one meal of edible chrysanthemum, for example, though it was all right – and some are gorged on till we're sick of them for a few years. But that's part of the fun of it.

Put all these together with the perennial vegetables listed earlier, and the staples in Chapter 2, and you've got a year of good eating.

The box garden

A lot of veg in a very small space

Get a styrofoam box from the supermarket.
- Half fill it with weeds or lawn clippings or cabbage leaves, etc.
- Fill the rest with potting mix or compost or even garden soil. (Cook it in the oven first for half an hour to kill weed seeds.)
- Bung in some seedlings.

You can fit a lot of plants in a styrofoam box. Say: six lettuce, one cucumber, and three silverbeet plants, or a couple of silverbeet and a tomato or zucchini that will sprawl over the edge so it doesn't take up too much room; or six parsley plants, a capsicum, a come-and-come-again lettuce (one you just pull the leaves off as you want them), and a cucumber trailing out of the box – the variety is endless. You can also put your box next to a post and let climbing beans trail up it.

Salad box

This year we have a salad box outside the back door. It gets the green water which has steamed the veg (we don't use salt, and leftover vegetable water is good fertiliser), cold tea-leaves, coffee grounds, leftover herbal tea

tomato

lettuce

zucchini

The Box Garden.

detritus, and anything else that's convenient to throw out the back door, like the dirt from the dust pan. (This is high in both nitrogen and phosphorous – most dust is, with bits of hair and skin as well, which is excellent fertiliser.)

In the box we've got parsley and chives, a cut-and-come-again lettuce (cos will do), a cucumber, a rainbow chard plant (the young leaves are good in salads), Egyptian mint (very mild, and good chopped in tabouli), and a tiny Tim tomato which I either keep pruned or let sag over the edge.

The box certainly doesn't keep us in salads, but it can provide a meal when it is dark or raining and I don't want to trudge down to the vegetable garden – and it makes an excellent Christmas present for an elderly friend.

You can cram a lot in a box because plants can lean over the edge of it – you only need enough room for the roots. As long as you water it, and feed it with soluble fertiliser every day (either commercial seaweed-based fertiliser or home-made 'throw weeds, comfrey, compost, manure, and urine in a bucket, cover with water, then wait a week and ladel it out' fertiliser – otherwise known as brown gunge).

One box can provide two lettuces a week, four feeds of silverbeet, three harvests of celery, a couple of cucumbers and parsley. Best of all: you can grow it where you can reach it whenever you need a handful of greens.

Chapter 4

Fruit for all seasons

Any Australian household should be able to eat home-grown fruit the year round: at least three different sorts at any time of the year. This is, in fact, what many people used to do. Nowadays we've forgotten how easy it is to grow our own fruit, and we're often no longer familiar with old-fashioned and non-commercial varieties that once gave us bountiful harvests.

Why grow your own fruit?

Because it's fun. Because it tastes good.

Because one case of commercial fruit costs about $15 wholesale, so you'll save at least $1,000 a year. (And that pays for quite a range of fruit trees and bushes.)

Because there is something magic about being able to go into the backyard and simply pick whatever you need for the following days.

Because a backyard full of heavy grapevines, rich red strawberries, golden kiwi fruit, and trees laden with apples is beautiful and smells like heaven.

Because you'll never again have to walk past peaches at $2 each, or past costly avocados or punnets of overpriced strawberries, thinking 'Can I afford it?'.

It's hard to feel broke with cases of fruit in the laundry; with the smell of ripe fruit lingering round the back steps; with ever-present baskets-full of fruit to give away to friends. Maybe self-sufficiency is the wrong term. Growing your own is a form of generosity to yourself, to the birds and bees and insects that will also feed on your bounty, and to everyone around you.

How to grow enough fruit

A good fruit tree should give you four to six cases of fruit. Ten or twelve fruit trees will give you sixty cases of fruit – more than one case per week.

Even small gardens should be able to fit in twelve fruit trees. Most gardens, in fact, can fit in twenty or thirty trees, if they are grown as a tall hedge around the fence line. Forget about neat orchard spacing – that is mostly for the convenience of the machines that tend them. Cram your trees together, no more than 2 metres apart. This way they'll grow tall and tangle together, but they won't give any less fruit. (The birds won't find the fruit so easily either.) I try and alternate deciduous trees with evergreens like citrus and avocados: the evergreen fruit is ripening when the deciduous trees have lost their leaves.

Grow 'small fruits' like blueberries and rhubarb and strawberries underneath your fruit trees and around the edges. These are originally understory fruits and will tolerate semi-shade. Consider berries, passionfruit, grapes and kiwi fruit along the fence, up tall posts or pergolas.

Consider dwarf fruit trees too – grow them as a hedge. Dwarf peaches and nectarines can be kept trimmed knee-high along a path. Hazelnuts and almonds can be kept pruned as short as you want them. Dwarf apples are taller, but they crop within a couple of years.

What trees to plant

When I first became interested in self-sufficiency I planted any edible fruit I could find: Russian 'olives' and Irish strawberries, Brazilian cherries and cherry guavas. We now have about 120 sorts of fruit in our garden – still, we mostly only eat staples like apples, citrus, plums and peaches.

Plant the fruit you like to eat. In a small garden I would have four apples (late, medium and early), three oranges (at least one valencia and one navel), one mandarin, two lemons (summer and winter bearing), a multigraft pear and a multigraft cherry. Then two peaches (late and early), two plums (ditto), one nectarine and two avocados (if you can grow them in your area). But if grapefruit are your passion, you should grow them instead.

For 'soft fruit' I would grow two passionfruit vines (we eat a lot of passionfruit), three grape-vines (these take up almost no room if you grow them twined up a tall pole), one male and one female kiwi fruit, as many strawberries as you can fit beneath your trees, six blueberries, a bed of raspberries, and a trellis full of brambleberries.

This would give our family a basic supply. After that I'd look at 'luxury' trees: chestnuts (kept pruned small), mulberries, loquats for early fruit, tamarillos, grapefruit, quinces (because it's hard to buy a good quince), medlars, and dozens of others. But how much fruit you eat, and what sort, is a very personal thing. Every household's tastes are different.

Dwarf Fruit-tree hedge

Some unusual fruit

One of the advantages of growing your own is that you don't have to stick to commercial varieties, which are often chosen because they store and travel well – not because they are the tastiest. (One of our best apples here is Irish peach: delicious, but not red and dramatic enough to be saleable.)

Be adventurous in your choice of fruit. Avocados aren't a common garden tree, but they can be grown as far south as Melbourne along a warm, north-facing wall. (We grow ours here in 5 degrees of frost!) If you like tamarillos, plant one: tall tamarillo shrubs will grow from seed. Try limes instead of lemons – they're just as easy to grow, even if they are more expensive. Remember that you can keep tall trees pruned to fit your garden, and that if you plant them closely together they'll be tall and lanky anyway. Don't just buy the first apple at the nursery – take time to track down the varieties you like.

I regularly visit to the best, most exotic fruit shop in Canberra, where I buy any new fruit to come onto the market. If I like it, I plant the seed. This way we now have varieties of grapes, olives, oranges, loquats, tamarillos, avocados, peaches and apples which otherwise we may never have been able to track down or afford. The result may not be completely true to type – but, so far it has always been good, and near enough for our own use.

Successions

Always try to plant one early, one late and one medium variety of all your favourite fruits. We grow Gravenstein apples for January, then Jonathans, Cox's Orange Pippin and Golden Delicious, with Granny Smiths and Lady Williams for late eating. Navel oranges fruit in winter, valencias in summer. We start the peach season with tiny white peaches in December, and finish with Golden Queens in March. 'One of each' is not enough when you're growing your own: you really need to spread out your varieties.

Early and late fruit

Anyone can have abundant fruit in summer and autumn. It is harder to have plenty of fruit in late winter, and even harder to have spring fruit – especially if your area is too cold for citrus, avocados and other evergreens.

This is where early and late croppers come in. Late-bearing fruit trees include Lady Williams apples (pick them from May to June), medlars, quinces and pomegranates which only turn sweet after a frost. Kiwi fruit will crop in hot to cold areas, and the fruit will ripen all through winter.

Loquats are the earliest cropper: they flower in winter, even in cold areas, and give masses of sweet spring fruit. Loquats don't travel well, and you rarely see them in shops – but as kids we loved them. They are good stewed too.

Strawberries are one of the first spring fruits, as are early varieties of raspberries. Grow your strawberries on black weed mat to speed up cropping. We grow some of ours on weed mat under the apple trees – and the berries have fruit by the time the trees are in leaf. Most small berries are early ripeners.

Other early fruit includes gooseberries, early raspberries, banana passionfruit and cherries.

Growing 'warm climate' fruit in cold areas

Most fruit-growing advice for gardeners is based on commercial practice. No-one would grow custard apples commercially near Melbourne – but you can grow one or two with a bit of effort. Many fruit trees are much more tolerant than we've been lead to believe.

Many 'warm climate' fruits will tolerate frozen ground, but not wind or late frosts.

To enable you to grow a far greater variety of fruit, try the following techniques:

- mulch your trees in late winter to retard blossoming;
- spray with a weekly seaweed or nettle spray for greater cold-resistance;
- add potash to the soil in autumn to 'harden' new growth; and
- use plastic tree-guards for the first couple of years.

Grow 'warm climate' fruit in the following places:

- on north-facing slopes;
- against a north-facing or courtyard wall (brick or stone, or insulated wood);
- near a large dam or body of water;
- against the north face of a large boulder;
- in a grove of other trees for greater frost protection and insulation; or
- in a greenhouse.

Storing fruit

If you have trees cropping throughout the year, you won't need to store much fruit. Fruit will of course keep longer in the fridge. We store apples through spring, wrapped in newspaper in a cool shed. The old-fashioned way to store apples or grapes was in bran in a barrel, or underground in an earthen cellar. Look for the new storage bags that slowly release ethylene – the gas that ripens fruit. They really do work.

Citrus can be stored after 'half drying'. Put them in the sun till they start to shrivel. Make sure they don't get wet. Then store them in a very dry place, not touching each other and away from any other fruit.

I've kept oranges this way for up to two years. They become hard and thin-skinned – but the inside is still juicy and sweet. I find though that commercial citrus can rarely be kept this way – perhaps they're too prone to rot because they're grown with too much high-nitrogen fertiliser.

Spreading the harvest

Commercial orchards like to harvest all their fruit at the same time. For them, that's more efficient. But the home gardener does better with the crop spread over several weeks. You can do this by:
- Planting trees close together, to minimise sunlight: the top fruit ripens first, the bottom fruit several weeks later.
- Minimum pruning: thick, leafy branches have the same result as close planting.
- Choosing a wide range of early and late varieties (say, Lady Sudely and Lady Williams apples: the first ripens in December/January, the latter can be picked in late July).
- Using micro-climates.

Micro-climates

Even a small garden has warm and cold areas. In my garden two Golden Delicious apple trees flower and bear two weeks apart – one is in a warm spot, the other in a frosty hollow. Such micro-climates can be utilised not only to extend the growing season of your fruit, but also to extend the range of fruit you grow: a frost hollow may give enough chilling for apples, a warm, sheltered spot by a north-facing wall may let you grow avocados.

Warm areas include north-facing walls – preferably white-washed, which reflect, and stone walls, which store the heat. Often, spots by dams or fish ponds are warmer – the water stores heat. You can also make a 'warm' garden by piling up old tyres a couple of metres, filling them with compost, and growing crops in them. North-facing slopes are usually less frosty, as are the higher areas of the garden.

Cold spots are often hollows, where the frost can't drain away, exposed sites with cold winds, and shady spots without much direct sunlight – especially the warm morning light.

Wander round your orchard at different times of the year. Some places will feel warmer, some cooler. Mark them on a chart and adjust your planting accordingly.

Feeding your trees

Well-fed trees produce more. They also tend to have fewer pests and less disease. If you doubt this, do a trial: feed one tree well, and ignore its neighbour – and count the bugs over a period of a few years.

The easiest fruit tree feeding regime is mulch. One good mulch per year is enough for a mature tree; one in spring and one in autumn suits a young tree. If you feel your trees need more feeding, scatter hen manure or blood & bone on top of the mulch. It will also help the mulch to break down faster.

If you don't like the look of mulched trees, just scatter on the blood & bone or manure in late spring and early autumn, and keep the grass under the trees well mown – or grow berries instead of grass: they will provide natural mulch each winter as their leaves drop off.

Pruning

Pruning is one of the more individual aspects of gardening. Few growers agree about pruning. I prune very little – but then, I am not interested in maximising my yields. Unpruned trees generally produce smaller fruit, but more of it, and the harvest continues over a longer time. Commercial growers can't afford this. Fruit must be big, ripen within a ten-day period and be easily visible. If my fruit were easily visible, the bower birds would grab it before I could.

The exception to this are peaches and almonds. They bear only on the previous season's growth. Most peaches need to be pruned to get a good crop. But there are old trees in our orchard that haven't been pruned for twenty years and still bear luscious, white-fleshed fruit. Perhaps old varieties are more tolerant – and any vigorous tree will of course keep growing, so there will always be some new fruiting wood. However, the general rule is to cut back older peach wood to encourage new growth and stimulate dormant buds.

Whenever you are tempted to prune, always remember: the vigour of a plant or branch depends on its leaf surface – plants photosynthesise, and without leaves they can't. On the other hand, with most fruit trees great masses of leaves mean a poorer crop, with poorer keeping qualities. So don't bung on high-nitrogen fertiliser just to increase the leaf area.

If you are tempted to cut out those high-reaching branches, remember: the nearer a shoot approaches a vertical position, the more vigorous it is.

The greatest plant growth takes place at the top buds, and then decreases the further down you go. High-growing branches are more vigorous – and anyway, wallabies, goats, and other foragers can't reach the fruit up there. On the other hand, neither can you, without a good ladder or energetic kids.

The more severely you prune young trees the longer it will take them to fruit. Open or vase-shaped trees are easy to spray and harvest – but their structure may be weaker and their shape will be much less beautiful. Unless you need to squeeze out ever piece of fruit you can, just let the poor babies grow.

Trees have fruited comfortably for thousands of years without our interference – after all, that's how they reproduce. It is one of the great human fallacies that we always have to jump in and control things to get the best results – in this case, to get any crop at all.

Staple fruit all year round

Staple fruit are the backbone of your garden. If you have apples and citrus for fresh eating and cooking, berries for luxury, and avocados and nuts for protein, you have a good basis for self-sufficiency.

A year of apples

Most of the apples we eat today are cold-store apples – floury, and tasting of storage instead of the sun. The varieties we buy are limited to those that store and travel well, and have a bright, fresh colour, even when they're stale.

It's possible to have apples ripening in your garden for eight months of the year – and then to have them stored for the other four months. But to do this you have to go beyond the conventional Golden Delicious/Granny Smith range we're so used to. Actually, doing that has a bonus: the juiciest, tartiest and most fragrant apples aren't necessarily the ones that travel best.

A century ago there were hundreds of apple varieties available in Australia. Gradually the range has narrowed. The same apple varieties now grow from Tasmania to Southern Queensland. If asked, most children today would only know the name of two or three apples – probably Grannie Smith, Jonathan or Golden Delicious – or they may just tell you 'red' and 'green'.

Finding and choosing your apples

Nurseries do need to stock the 'popular' apples to satisfy demand, but any good nursery will have less common varieties as well – and may well be prepared to order in others for the next season, or even to bud ones especially for you.

Large nurseries may have parent trees from which a graft can be taken, and will take orders a year or so in advance. There are also various nurseries that specialise in old-fashioned trees. The one I usually use is Badger's Keep in Chewton, Victoria. They have an excellent mail order service, and over three hundred varieties are for sale.

Alternatively, you can raise your own rootstock from seed, or locate the varieties you want and either learn to bud or graft yourself or hire someone to do it for you. Most nurseries will be able to help you with this. Although it might be an unusual request, it is one most professionals would be interested in.

Even if you don't want to grow your own, scout around the district for neglected trees in old orchards, wild apple trees on the side of the road, or big old trees near farmhouses. You may well find varieties you never dreamed of whilst munching a Granny Smith from the supermarket.

To get a long apple harvest, you need to choose early varieties that start fruiting in December to January, and late varieties that fruit in June.

The three earliest apples available in Australia are Joaneting, Lady Sudely and Abas. Joaneting is a crisp apple when picked, but it goes soft quickly. It should be eaten straight from the tree. It will ripen in late December to early January. Lady Sudely is a better choice, though it ripens a couple of weeks later. The fruit is large, striped and very sweet. Unlike these two relatively unknown apples, Abas is available at most nurseries. It's a soft, sweet apple with striped fruit and a tendency to biennial bearing.

In warm areas with cool winters (so the apples set fruit) Joaneting and Lady Sudely may mature in December, with Abas a couple of weeks later.

Gravenstein is another very early apple. Traditional Gravensteins are small and mostly yellow. Red Gravenstein is a more modern cultivar – it is bright red with deeper red stripes, and seems to be larger than the traditional variety. Gravensteins should mature in early to late January, depending on your climate.

Cox's Orange Pippin has been described as the world's best tasting apple. It is red striped and not as appetising to look at as Delicious, for example, but crisp and sweet and fragrant. It matures before the bulk of the main season apples: Johnathons, Delicious (or the slightly earlier Red Delicious), and Golden Delicious.

An old-fashioned but still easily obtainable variety is Five Crown Pippin. This is a very heavy cropper, with large, flat yellow-green fruit. It is best suited to very cold areas.

Starkrimson is an apple tree for harsh conditions: drought, flood, wind, or heavy frost – Starkrimson should survive.

In warmer areas, where apples traditionally won't grow, a good mid-season apple is Lalla, or Red Delicious. It is very like its parent Delicious, but a much deeper red, all over.

Very late apples are crucial to anyone wanting a year's supply of apples. The traditional late apple is Granny Smith, which will keep until the Gravensteins come in. But there are later ones, including the Granny Smith derivative Lady Williams. This doesn't mature until at least mid-June, and often later, so you may still be picking apples at the end of July. It is a large red apple, very crisp and slightly acid – and, of course, very long-keeping. The trees usually give enormous crops. It is one of the most delicious apples I know, and keeps its flavour wonderfully.

Rome Beauty matures weeks after Granny Smith. It is firm and a good bearer. Rome Beauty is also a reasonable cooking apple, though not as flavourful as Granny Smith, and harder and not as sweet when eaten fresh.

Stayman's Winesap is now less well known, but it was once much more popular. It is an American cultivar, very firm – a red apple with darker stripes and scented, slightly acid flesh.

Yates is an old-fashioned late apple that used to be much more popular before apple varieties were 'rationalised' into a few choice lines. It is a very small red apple, very sweet and firm. It originated in the USA and, like many of the late apples, it is a very heavy bearer.

Northern Spry shouldn't be picked before mid-June, and may even be cropping at the end of July. It is a very popular apple in the USA and is often used as a rootstock in Australia, so it should be available even if nurseries don't advertise it. The fruit isn't large and tends to bruise – not an apple to display in the fruiterer's, and one of the reasons it isn't commercially popular here – but it is very sweet and fragrant.

Don't rely on bearing dates too closely: a lot will depend on your particular climate, the position of your tree in the garden, and how open the tree is from pruning. Cool summers may also mean later fruit – which can ripen extraordinarily rapidly as soon as the weather warms up.

Cooking apples

Don't neglect cooking apples either. For years I neglected the 'wild' apples growing round here – the ones planted generations ago and still bearing – no longer pruned because they aren't modern varieties and their value has been mostly forgotten. They looked gross to my inexperienced eye: too massive, too corpulent. A random bite didn't improve matters: they seemed tasteless and much too floury.

It was only when I was served the best apple crumble of my life at a neighbour's – made with 'twenty ouncers', a very old variety – that I realised these were cooking, not dessert apples: a category I'd never seen advertised in the fruit shops, and mostly ignored in the fruit tree catalogues, even by large suppliers.

I became a devotee of cooking apples like the English Bramleys, the classic cooking apple which explodes into sweet flouriness when baked. Or King Cole, an old Australian cultivar dating from the beginning of the century. It is very like a Jonathan: red, firm and juicy, but with the capacity to pulp finely and easily, and keep its flavour when cooked. That is the real test of a cooking apple: whether the flavour dissipates with heat, or actually improves, to become subtle and highly scented. Granny Smith, Five Crown Pippin and Sturmer Pippin are 'dual purpose' apples – good for both cooking and eating – but they still can't compare with the specialised cookers of last century.

A year of citrus

Any area with no more than light frosts should be able to have citrus all year round. With a bit of extra work you can grow citrus in areas that have up to eight degrees of frost.

Citrus in hot areas

Citrus are heavy feeders. Many subtropical citrus trees are stunted by lack of food, as mulch breaks down quickly in warm climates. Feed them at least four times a year with old hen manure or pelletised hen manure and at least two mulches.

Citrus in hot areas are also attacked by sooty mould: black patches over the leaves which interfere with photosynthesis. Sooty mould grows on the sweet secretions of sap suckers like aphids. Spray sap suckers with white oil when the temperature is below 24° C and there's no blossom on the tree. (Don't spray the whole tree, just the bits with the pests.) Control ants with a thick layer of grease around the base of the trunk or with a skirt of sump-oil impregnated wool or rags. Dab woolly aphids with methylated spirits, or just squash them.

Citrus in cold areas

Grow your citrus against a north facing wall, protected from cold winds, or within a grove of well established evergreen trees. Use a tube of clear plastic sheeting to provide shelter during winter in the first two years, and to encourage growth in late autumn and early spring. To reduce frost damage, spray with seaweed spray, Earthcare 2000 (a commercial spray), or home-made nettle spray. (Cover the nettles with water and spray when the liquid is a weak-tea colour.) Give a sprinkle of potash or wood ash in late summer: potash deficient plants are more prone to frost damage.

Don't mulch around your trees in cold areas, as mulch will increase frost damage to the leaves. Instead, grow other plants underneath to reduce the likelihood of the ground freezing.

Plant your citrus deeply – deeper roots will be more protected from the frozen soil on the surface. Water every day – a lot of 'cold stress' is in fact moisture stress due to evaporation – and water the leaves as well.

Don't worry if your citrus turns pale yellow in winter – it will green up again when the weather warms up.

Valencia oranges are more cold tolerant than Navels, and Seville oranges, though sourer, are more cold tolerant than Valencias. Citrons are more cold tolerant than lemons, though Meyer lemons can be grown in a large pot and taken indoors in winter. The bush lemon is the most cold hardy citrus of all. This is the warty, thick-skinned 'wild citrus'.

Some unusual citrus

Blood and Seville oranges	These resemble Valencia oranges, though they are more salt tolerant. There are several Blood orange varieties in Australia. The Rough Seville tastes like a slightly sweeter grapefruit and can be split into segments like a mandarin. The juice is slightly more palatable than grapefruit juice – it is quite nice fresh. Rough Sevilles are flat fruited, very vigorous and more tolerant of colder, dryer and wetter conditions than ordinary oranges.

	The Smooth Seville resembles the Rough Seville except that its skin is smooth and that it isn't always as vigorous.
Chinotto	This is an ornamental tree with small, 'smoky' fruit. It is very cold tolerant.
Bergamot	The Bergamot is probably a hybrid between a Seville orange and a lime. It is grown, mostly in Italy, for the oil from its skin for the perfume industry. However, it makes an excellent fragrant marmalade and anyone who can tolerate the sourness of a fresh grapefruit will find Bergamot a slightly sweeter, very refreshing fruit.
Lime	These are slightly less cold tolerant than lemons. They are also less vigorous and smaller trees, which can be grown in pots in a sheltered courtyard or crammed between other trees. They aren't as long lived as lemons. The most common lime in Australia is the West Indian lime. It should be harvested when it's still pale green – as soon as it lightens from dark green – or much of the delicate lime flavour will be lost. Don't wait for it to turn lemon yellow. On the other hand, in cold areas such as ours the limes turn yellow with a light frost or cold snap, and should be picked then.
Pummelo	These resemble thick skinned, very hardy grapefruit. They have a higher heat requirement than grapefruit, and are a good substitute for those in tropical or semi-tropical areas.
Citron	The Citron is one of the earliest cultivated fruits, and is mentioned in the Bible. Its peel, exquisitely fragrant, was once used extensively for candied peel. The dried peel can also be used as a moth repellent to protect both clothes and food.
	The Citron looks like a bulbous, rough skinned lemon – not to be confused with the Bush lemon, which is rounder and squatter. They have a thick pith and a slightly sweeter flesh than a lemon. Although it is said not to be quite as frost resistant as a lemon, I have found our specimen to be much hardier. It is a small tree which grows to about 4 metres high and, with frequent picking, seems constantly in fruit.
Tangelo	These are a delicious, thin skinned, deep coloured cross between a mandarin and a grapefruit – without the sickly sweetness of the one or the tartness of the other. They will tolerate light frost, and we have found them more drought resistant than oranges in the same area.
Kumquats	These are grown as ornamentals, though the fruit is thin skinned and sweet. Don't confuse them with the similar Calamondin which has sour fruit.
Australian Desert lime	This is an incredibly hardy tree: drought, heat and frost tolerant, it bears its fruit eight weeks from flowering. The fruit is kumquat sized, lime coloured and varies in sweetness and fragrance according to the cultivar. It has been hybridised with several citrus species.
Finger lime	This is an Australian tropical to sub-tropical rainforest tree with long, deep-green fruit. They are very acid.
	There are several other native Australian limes. None are commercially available to my knowledge, although stock might possibly be obtained on application from the Department of Agriculture.
Bush lemon	Bush lemons are really citronelles: rough skinned, many seeded and thick pithed. They are very drought and cold tolerant but short lived, except

where drainage is excellent. If your area is too dry or cold for other citrus try a citronelle. Either grow it from seed or ask a nursery to get one in for you. As it is a common rootstock it should be easy to obtain at a year's notice.

Year round citrus

January	Valencia orange, Eureka lemon, kumquat, grapefruit
February	Kumquat, grapefruit, Valencia orange, Eureka lemon
March	Kumquat, Valencia orange, grapefruit, Eureka lemon
April	Lime, kumquat, grapefruit, mandarin, lemons (several sorts), Leng Navel orange, Valencia orange
May	Lime, citron, kumquat, mandarins (several sorts), Leng Navel orange, Valencia orange
June	Lime, tangelo, citron, grapefruit, mandarin, lemon (Lisbon, Late Lane, Eureka or Meyer), Washington Navel orange
July	Lime, tangelo, grapefruit, mandarin (Ellendale), lemon, Washington Navel orange
August	Lime, tangelo, grapefruit, mandarin, Meyer lemon, Navel or Valencia oranges
September	Lime, tangelo, grapefruit, mandarin, Meyer lemon, Lisbon lemon, Valencia or Navel oranges
October	Lime, tangelo, grapefruit, Kara mandarin, Late Lane Navel orange, Valencia orange
November	Lime, tangelo, grapefruit, lemon, Late Lane Navel orange, Valencia orange
December	Lime, tangelo, kumquat, grapefruit, lemon, Late Lane Navel orange, Valencia orange

A year of Avocados

Avocados mean protein and luxury – and something to swap or give away to your friends. With a bit of planning they can be a year round staple: avocado on buttered toast in winter, cold avocado soufflé, avocado stuffed in chicken, avocado soup. When you have plenty of avocados, the list of what you can do with them expands indefinitely.

Most Australians can grow their own avocados. In fact, the avocado tree is badly misunderstood. Most gardening advice is based on commercial growing practices – and whilst you would never dream of having a commercial avocado orchard in Melbourne or Canberra, you can in fact grow a couple of avocado trees there, provided you're prepared to work at it.

More than anything else, avocados need shelter from the wind – and from direct sun in summer during the first years of their life. Put your avocado in a hessian shelter until it's taller than you. In cold areas, grow it against a north-facing wall or in a grove of trees. Don't mulch in winter – you'd increase frost damage on the leaves – and grow masses of herbs and small plants around it, or just let the grass grow up. Hass (the dark, black knobby ones) are fairly cold tolerant, but other cold tolerant varieties are coming on to the market.

Try growing your own from seed – they sprout readily. Grow a dozen or so, and see which ones do best. You need two compatible avocados to fruit. In small areas you could try growing them in the same hole, so their trunks twist. Avocados can be pruned to small hedges – but in the garden they are best left to grow tall, to maximise their fruiting area.

Picking

Avocados don't ripen until you pick them or until they fall off the tree. Even immature avocados will ripen – they just won't be as nutty and rich. You can start picking your young fruit as soon as it is apricot sized – or leave them on the tree until they fall. This way, even two trees will give you avocados most of the year – and four trees should definitely give you a full year of avocados.

Ripening times

These are the times that commercial avocados are picked. You can extend these times by at least three months either way through early and late picking, as discussed before.

Mid-March	Jalna
April	Jalna
May	Jalna, Zutano, Bacon
June	Zutano, Bacon, Fuerte
July	Zutano, Bacon, Fuerte, Rincon
August	Fuerte, Rincon, Edranol, Sharwill
September	Fuerte, Rincon, Edranol, Sharwill, Hazzard, Hass, Millicent
October	Rincon, Edranol Sharwill, Hass, Millicent
November	Sharwill, Hazzard, Hass, Millicent
December	Hazzard, Hass, Millicent

A year of nuts

Nuts are a classic survival food. They can be stored for years – and certainly at least until your trees crop again the following year.

The number of nut trees you need will vary enormously. It depends on whether you rely on them for part of your protein, or whether you just want them for nibbling or to put into cakes. Two almonds (or a double-graft almond) and one other nut tree will be enough for most households – but once you've got the nuts they're never wasted. I would grow as many as you can accommodate. Try a hedge of hazelnuts in cold areas, or a trimmed hedge of macadamias in warmer spots.

Nut milk

Nutmilk can be made the same way as soybean milk: soak the nuts for at least 24 hours. Pour off the water, cover with boiling water and blend in a blender or processor – blend well, continuing for several minutes after the grounds appear to be fine.

Pour the liquid through a sieve, pressing well. Use at once, sweeten if required, or boil it for two minutes to 'pasteurise' it. Bottle and seal, and it should keep for a week or two in the fridge. Almond milk is good, but make sure you peel the almonds or it will be bitter. Coconut milk can be made with ground coconut, though this will be richer and different from the milk of green coconuts. Hazelnut milk is rich too, but makes a tasty milk jelly. We used to use the residue, toasted in the oven with a drizzle of honey, as the basis for muesli. Or you can add oil for a nut paste.

Almonds

You need two varieties of almond to cross-pollinate. You will also need to prune your trees once they stop growing: almonds fruit on 1-year-old wood. Plant them in a well drained spot. Feed and water them well, although almonds are drought hardy if necessary. They need chilling to set fruit, so they aren't suited to hot areas, but the flowers – and even the trees – can be killed by late spring frosts.

Bunya nuts

The Bunya pine is a tall, wide, native tree, extremely imposing but not suited to small gardens. It grows slowly, fruiting only after 10 to 20 years, and may not fruit every year. It can be grown wherever you can grow a lemon tree.

The Bunya pine produces enormous pine cones, weighing up to 12 kilos, with the nuts, up to thumb size, contained in the cone. You'll need a hammer to husk them, and probably gloves too, as the cones are sticky inside.

An easier way to remove the nuts is to drop them in a hot fire (the way we did as kids) and wait for the first seeds to start shooting out. Pull the cone from the fire and rescue the rest of the fruit. Alternatively, you can try the same process in the oven, set at about 200° C for about ten minutes. Once you hear a nut explode, take the cone out at once.

Using Bunya nuts

Bunya nuts can be eaten straight from the cone or roasted in the oven. I have tried them fried in a little oil with garlic – very good – or with ground black pepper.

Bunya flour is made by boiling the nuts in their husks for twenty minutes, then hulling them, drying them and grinding them. Use the meal for cakes and pastry, like almond meal.

To store Bunya nuts husk them, dry them in the sun for a day, then place in sealed, dry jars until you need them. Alternatively, simply store the cones in a dry place where the rats can't get at them.

Growing Bunyas

Bunya trees are either male or female. Ostensibly you need both to produce nuts, though I have known females to bear when there is no male in the vicinity.

Grow the trees from seed – patiently, as they take about a year to germinate. The seed should be planted point down in moist soil and kept warm. The trees quickly develop a long tap root. Allow for this when you are planting them out, and transplant them carefully.

The young trees are prickly, and stock usually leave them alone. But they can be knocked back by frost, and some protection is needed for the first few years in frosty areas. Make sure the young trees are kept moist and free of weeds and grass: in the wild they grow in bare ground under a parent tree, and you should try to duplicate this.

Cashews

These are a tropical tree, but have been known to grow as far south as the south coast of New South Wales: with care, in a very sheltered frost-free spot. They need plenty of sun, and deep, rich, well drained soil with lots of moisture.

The cashew nuts themselves will be produced covered in a fleshy 'apple'. The apple is also edible, but its tastiness varies from tree to tree. *Never try to crack unprocessed cashew nuts*: the shells contain a bitter, caustic sap. To get rid of this, place the nuts under a thin layer of sand in an old metal tray. Make sure it is an old tray – the sap may stain it irrevocably. Put them in a hot oven of about 200°C for twenty minutes. The sap will spurt out of the nuts and be absorbed by the sand. Don't open the oven while this is going on, as some of the sap will vaporise. When it is finished, open the oven door and quickly go outside until the vapour has dissipated.

When the sand is cool take out the nuts – wearing gloves – and wash them in hot water with plenty of detergent to get rid of any remaining sap. Then crack the nuts and remove the flesh, peeling off the thin brown skin.

Roast the nuts in coconut or other oil (or in an oven bag for oil-less nuts) in the oven for five minutes at 150°C.

Warning: *don't touch your face or eyes while you are processing cashews.*

Chilean nut (*Gevuina avellana*)

This evergreen tree requires a temperate to sunny tropical climate. The nut is similar to a hazelnut, but sweeter and usually larger. It is usually eaten roasted. The Chilean nut grows to 7 metres high and is a good wind break.

Hazelnuts

These can reach 7 metres if grown by themselves – they are much smaller when planted thickly for a hedge. Hazelnuts will tolerate cold to temperate climates. Seedlings can take many years to flower: grafting them onto suckers produces better results. Two varieties are needed for good pollination.

Macadamias

We grow macadamias here (southern NSW), with up to five degrees frost. The macadamias aren't worried by this, so they probably tolerate colder conditions as long as they are surrounded by other trees – like ours are – to protect them from cold winds. Macadamias grow slowly from seed, or you can buy a grafted one. They prefer moist, fertile soil.

Pecans

These are enormous trees – but if you prune off the lower branches, you will have room for other plants below. Knock off the ripe nuts with a long stick. Pecans need deep, fertile, moist soil.

Pistachios

This tree tolerates drought, frost, and poor soil, although it grows better without them. Pistachios thrive wherever olives can grow. In good conditions the trees grow up to ten metres tall. You need at least one male to every six female pistachio trees. Propagate them by seed and grafting.

Walnuts

Walnuts need deep, fertile soil. They can grow to be enormous and aren't really suitable for backyards. But they tolerate heavy pruning, so they could be grown on the footpath.

Ten months of berries

Berries crop quickly and are low growing. Both characteristics make them valuable for the home grower.

With a little extra work – and a careful choice of varieties – you can be eating home-grown berries throughout temperate and most of 'cold' Australia for ten months of the year. The only equipment you need are plastic cloches: plastic strung over your berries to shelter them from frost in autumn and to get them growing quickly in spring. Even without cloches late raspberries will still be cropping in a sheltered position in Canberra in July, and early strawberries will be fruiting by October. In frost-free areas 'winter' strawberries will crop from May through to November.

Using surplus berries

Except for strawberries, berries can be dried. Soak to reconstitute them, then stew them. Or you can dry them very slowly in the oven until crisp. If the oven is too hot they'll turn brown, so they should retain at least some original colour. Dried like this, you can grind them for berry flour. This can be added to cakes, biscuits, bread, and so on as a sweetener – or added to honey to make fruit honey. Berry flour is also lovely added to custard.

Instead of berry jam, make preserved berries. Boil sugar or honey with water until it just sets in a saucer of cold water. Add an equal quantity of berries – say one cup of berries to one cup of the liquid. Bring this to the boil, then take it off again at once, and bottle and seal. The berries should keep their shape with the liquid just coloured from their juice. Store this preserve in the fridge until you want it.

Brandied berries are luxurious. Combine one cup of berries with one cup of sugar and one of brandy. Bottle and seal, and leave it for at least three months before using. Gin is also good instead of brandy – especially with strawberries and raspberries. Whisky is lovely with strawberries, port great fun with blackberries.

Strawberries

Maximising your crop
You have two choices: firstly, you can have conventional, slightly raised and rounded beds and cover them with cloches as soon as the leaves begin to turn on the trees, and then leave the cloches there until the fruit sets. This will stop the last of the berries being frosted off, and protect the crowns and early blossom.

Make your own cloches with bent-over old coathangers covered in clear plastic bags. The plastic will only last one season – but it is easily replaced next time you go to the supermarket.

Alternatively, forget about conventional strawberry beds altogether and grow your berries under trees. After all, strawberries are originally an under-tree forest species, and do well in broken light, sheltered by the trees and fertilised by fallen leaves. You can also create your own forest effect: I've grown strawberries under a pergola of kiwi fruit, whilst a neighbour just rambled hers as groundcover through the flower beds. This was a very successful combination: the perennial flowers protected the strawberries, and the strawberries kept weeds from the flowers – and the berries were much less obvious to the birds.

Other means of maximising strawberries:
- Mulch – either natural mulch as leaves fall over the beds, or deliberate mulching. Black plastic gives excellent results as long as summer isn't too hot – shallow-rooted strawberries can cook or be burnt by black plastic. Try combining black plastic in warm areas with a pergola, with a late-leafing cover like kiwi fruit or chokos. This way you will still have the early heating effect of the black plastic, but the fruit will be protected in mid-summer.
- Cut back. Try cutting back your strawberry plants as soon as the first burst of fruit is over. I use a whippersnipper, just running over them as

though I am mowing the grass. This will set the plants back so they will produce fewer runners – but they should recover in time for an autumn or even a winter crop. Even Red Gauntlet, which produces through most of the summer, can be cut back in early autumn and then cloched. That way you should get some berries in early winter.

- Raised tyre beds. Pile up old tyres about four high, fill them with compost or good soil with a little compost on top, and plant your strawberries so they trail over the edge. The high garden will be less prone to frost, and the black tyres will absorb and store heat. One warning though: these raised tyre gardens need extra watering, particularly if filled with water-loving strawberries.
- Feed only with continuous mulch, applied in late spring when the ground has warmed up and in mid-summer if necessary.
- Plant several varieties, even one or two which aren't really suited to your area – unseasonal conditions may suit them some years, when even a few winter or early spring strawberries are welcome.

How many plants?
About 100 plants should give two adults and two children several meals of strawberries a week. Strawberry lovers should have at least 1,000 plants. This may seem a lot – but 1,000 plants take up surprisingly little room when planted round your trees.

Cultivation
Strawberries prefer acid soil – mulch is almost a necessity, and a pine or casaurina needle mulch is excellent. If you get less than 25 mm of rain a week you'll need to water your strawberries – in which case, 'dome' the bed so that excess moisture doesn't pond.

If you mulch your berries, or grow them under the trees where they get each year's leaf litter, you may not have to feed your berries at all. Otherwise give them a scatter of blood & bone or old hen manure in winter.

Strawberries tend to dry out, and will burn in extreme heat. Grow them under a pergola in hot areas. In cold areas, mulch them well so they get an early start, and cover them with hessian in early spring to keep the early flowers from burning off.

Plant your runners in autumn or winter – autumn planting is more usual in sub-tropical areas where a winter crop is wanted. Set the runners out on their own small hills, or just plant them about a handspan apart.

Buy virus-tested runners – next door's spares are probably virus infested, and won't bear well. The virus is spread by aphids, and commercial growers replace runners every three years because plants are usually infected by then. But the home gardener, who doesn't mind a smaller yield, need not worry about this.

If you are choosing your own runners, try to take the first runner on a plant, and one that hasn't flowered yet. Thin out beds as they become crowded.

Many people use a black plastic mulch – you get both earlier and later fruit, fewer weeds and runners, and you need to water less – but strawberries can bake under black plastic in hot summers.

Pests
Strawberries are infected by a variety of leaf problems, all with much the same solutions. Try spraying bordeaux in winter, use trickle irrigation instead of over head sprinklers, don't let your beds get overcrowded, and keep mulching.

Varieties
I recommend at least a few bushes of Cambridge Vigour, one of the earliest fruiters which starts here (southern NSW) in September and continues through to Christmas. You also get a few autumn berries if you cut the plants back in January.

Tioga, Torrey and Naratoga are also early varieties, worth diversifying with. Red Gauntlet is one of the most popular strawberries. The fruit are large, though not as well-flavoured as others, and the bushes crop over a very long season. If you want just one variety, this is probably it.

In sub-tropical areas Redlands Crimson is the most important commercial variety, cropping from autumn through to spring.

Narbello is another long cropper, and Phenomenal is one of the most popular home varieties.

Strawberries from seed
Alpine strawberries grow from seed, don't produce runners and aren't attractive to birds. However, the fruit isn't particularly attractive to humans either. The texture is slightly cardboardy, and it isn't very sweet except in cold areas. But they do produce through winter under trees, even in cold climates like Canberra's, and provide at least something red to stick on mid-winter pavlovas.

Alpine strawberry seed is available from Thompson & Morgen through most nurseries and specialist suppliers. Sow the seed in spring. It grows quickly and easily, and makes a pretty groundcover under trees and shrubs, or around potted plants.

Blueberries

How many bushes?
Half a dozen to a dozen plants should be ample for a family, unless you love blueberry pie. Plant at least two varieties: one early, one late.

Planting
Choose varieties carefully – there are many on the market, some needing intense cold for the fruit to set, others better suited to temperate areas. Blueberries will grow in hot areas, but they don't taste of much. Bluecrop and Denise are early to mid-season, and Rose and Brigitta mid to

late-season varieties. Brigitta berries can be left unpicked for several weeks without deteriorating.

Space the plants between one and two metres apart – though commercial bushes are planted closer and thinned later – a good blueberry bush should grow about two metres wide. Plant them when they're dormant, or in pots at any time of the year.

Cultivation

Blueberries need a moist, acid soil with lots of humus, long, warm days and cool nights, and a six-month frost-free period, especially during January and February when the fruit is maturing. Blueberries are shallow-rooted and need moisture, mulch, and good drainage. If you use drip irrigation, spread the drippers out: blueberries are wide rooters and one dripper per plant won't be enough. Prune the young plants heavily to encourage bushy growth: cut away any weak growth, any frosted branches, and any dense, low growth. Also, cut out old wood (more than three years old) every year.

Mulch regularly, and scatter blood & bone or hen manure if needed – this will depend on the quality of your mulch – in late winter and after the fruit has set.

Picking

Blueberries fruit when they are between four and eight years old. A mature bush yields up to eight kilos of fruit. Let the fruit ripen on the bush: it won't get riper after it has been picked. Pick the fruit at least once a week.

Brambleberries

A range of brambleberries should give you fruit from November through to February, starting with loganberries, followed by youngberries, boysenberries and marionberries. Thornless loganberries are also available, as are thornless blackberries – these are less vigorous than the wild ones and fruit in late January – and silvanberries and lawtonberries.

Cultivation

In all but cold areas most brambles grow best in semi-shade: try them under fruit trees or a pergola. All are vigorous, need trellising (canes can grow up to four metres tall), and should keep fruiting for at least twenty years. Make sure you tie them up well to their stakes or they'll be sprawling everywhere.

Feed brambles in winter when you hack back excess growth: give them a thick cover of good compost or other mulch. That should be all they need.

Plant brambles in winter – just haul up bits of someone else's canes which have rooted themselves. Like blackberries, any bit of bramble covered by soil tends to root.

Problems

Birds love brambles, so grow enough for them too. Untidy brambles hide the fruit better. If fruit is spoiled by fungus, thin the canes out more in winter or, as a last resort, spray with bordeaux when they are dormant. The major problem with brambles though is excess growth.

Raspberries

There are literally dozens of raspberry varieties available from specialist nurseries. Some bear incredibly early, some incredibly late – there won't be much fruit, but it's there when you want it. Most common varieties produce large but fairly tasteless fruit. If you love raspberries I'd advise planting as many sorts as you can get hold of. We have about a dozen fruiting in our garden, but the labels are long vanished and I can't remember what they are.

If you are limited to readily available varieties try Skelna, Chilcotin and Heritage for a range of early, medium, and late fruit.

Always stake your raspberries, otherwise they'll wander all over the place. I just tie them up in bunches to star pickets with old pantyhose, rescued from public service friends.

Pruning

Different varieties of raspberry have different pruning needs, which have to be met for maximum yields. As a general rule, prune back early raspberries (those that fruit before Christmas) as soon as they have fruited. For other canes, cut out any that have fruited in winter.

Feeding

Mulch your raspberries, and replace the mulch whenever it thins out. This will not only feed the plants, but keep in moisture and keep down weeds – and raspberry plants are horrible, prickly things to have to weed around.

Propagating

Most raspberries produce several canes each year, and some varieties produce masses of them. Anyone who has been growing raspberries for a few years will happily swap some canes for something – and there are many raspberry addicts who grow delicious, old-fashioned varieties and are overjoyed to find appreciative homes for surplus canes.

Fruit for small places

Babaco	These long, golden fruit vaguely resemble pawpaw but are much more cold tolerant, growing naturally in the Andes with temperatures ranging between 0 and 20°C. They tolerate semi-shade, fruit within six months to two years, and need plenty of water and protection from sunburn. Try growing them under a pergola if the temperature rises above 25°C where you live. The tree is small, only two-and-a-half metres at the most and, like pawpaw, the fruits hang down from the top of the trunk. You can get about 70 fruit per tree, with each fruit weighing between 1 and 2 kilos. The trees should fruit well for eight to ten years.
	Pick the fruit when they are about 10 cm in diameter and are turning yellow instead of dark green.

Babacos like rich soil with a good humus content. They are propagated mostly from tissue culture as they do not produce seeds.

Cape gooseberry These aren't the same as traditional thorny gooseberries. They are small, frost sensitive bushes, which tolerate semi-shade. Perennial in warm climates, they readily re-seed elsewhere, grow easily from seed and fruit in one year. The fruit is held in transparent 'lanterns', bright yellow and slightly tart.

Gooseberries Gooseberries grow on small, deciduous bushes, about one metre high and wide, and very prickly. They tolerate semi-shade in warm areas and fruit in one to two years. The branches grow low to the ground and are usually pruned to the upward facing buds, with the centre kept open for easy picking among the thorns.

Gooseberries can be eaten green in pies, jam and chutney, or ripe when the fruit is bright red. Gooseberries are easily propagated by layering: just cover a branch with soil until it roots.

Gooseberries will grow in both very cold areas and temperate conditions. You can also grow them, with care, in hotter climates as long as you mulch heavily and don't let them dry out. Fruit set, however, may not be as good without frost in winter.

Mountain pawpaw This is a cool climate, bright yellow pawpaw and can be grown in all but the coldest areas of Australia. It tolerates semi-shade and crops in one year. The fruit is about 10 cm long and fragrant, but not as sweet as ordinary paw paw. You need both a male and a female tree.

Pepino These small bushes can be grown wherever tomatoes grow. The oval, yellow, or slightly striped fruit tastes slightly like a rich rockmelon. They crop in five months, in late autumn.

Tamarillo These are tree tomatoes. In warm areas they fruit all year, but around here, in southern NSW, you get a few in early spring, left over from autumn, then a major autumn or early winter crop. They tolerate a few degrees of frost and semi-shade. Tamarillos propagate from seed, cool weather cuttings, or by layering, and bear in one year.

Footpath trees

These are trees that no-one else will recognise as edible. Grow them along the footpath or on the nature strip, and no-one's likely to steal your fruit.

Jakfruit Though ostensibly a tropical tree, this will grow as far south as Ballina. It produces enormous, strongly flavoured fruit – too strong if the fruit is overripe – with a tough rind. The seeds can be peeled and used like breadfruit. The sawdust of the jakfruit tree can be boiled to produce a strong yellow dye, which is used by Buddhist monks in Asia to colour their robes.

Japanese raisin tree The fruit from this tree is not edible – it is the raisin-shaped bulbous twists in the stems that are sweet, often delicious, and tasting very like raisins.

The raisin tree will tolerate moderate though not heavy frost as well as hot conditions. It grows slowly to 18 metres, with deeply fissured bark and small white flowers. Propagate it by seed or cuttings from young branches.

Lilly pilly, Eugenia This is a small native tree, neatly shaped, and often seen in gardens or along footpaths. Its young foliage is frost tender but otherwise it does survive light frost, especially if it is grown in the shelter of larger trees. It needs moist soil, has white flowers and berries which range from green to blue to red, depending on the cultivar.

Lilly pilly fruit ranges from just edible to tasty: like most trees not selected for their fruit, its quality varies. But even at their least tasty, lilly pillies make excellent chutney: use an apple chutney recipe, and substitute half the apple quantity with lilly pillies.

Linden Linden trees tolerate heavy frost. Linden fruit can be made into jams or jellies, or stewed with sugar or honey. It makes a good sorbet: mix a sweetened puree with an equal quantity of whipped egg white, then freeze, stirring it twice as it sets.

Medlar This is an old-fashioned tree that lost popularity when people stopped growing their own fruit. It is a well-shaped, attractive, small tree (to six metres high), with lovely white flowers and small fruit, best eaten very ripe in early winter or late autumn when it is sweet, fragrant and soft. The leaves colour well in autumn. It is suitable for cold to sub-tropical areas, though the fruit won't be as well flavoured in the latter.

Narranjilla This orange, green-fleshed South African fruit is eaten fresh or juiced. The tree grows to one-and-a-half metres and suits tropical or sub-tropical conditions as far south as Sydney.

Pine nuts These come from the Swiss or the Mexican stone pine. Both are hardy and tolerate heat and cold as well as drought. The 'nuts' come from the ripe pine cones – let them scatter when the pines drop off the tree.

Pomegranate These are very hardy, attractive trees, suitable for cold to semi-tropical areas. The showy red flowers last for several weeks, the large red and yellow edible fruit is an excellent show piece for most of the rest of the year, hanging on the tree when the thin leaves have fallen after the first frost. Pomegranates can be scooped out to eat fresh or in fruit salads, or the seedy pulp can be used to make fragrant drinks.

Quandong This native tree grows in all mainland states. The fruit can be eaten fresh or stewed, and it makes good jam. Pick it when it starts to fall from the tree. The tree is a partial parasite and needs a good host tree – plant it in the middle of other bushes or near other trees.

White mulberry Unlike the black mulberry white mulberries are sweet even when immature, slightly honey tasting, and don't stain paving and clothes. The leaves are the traditional food for silkworms. White mulberry grows from cold to tropical conditions, drought tolerant once established, eventually incredibly long and deep rooted. Will grow slowly to about 18 metres but can be kept pruned.

Other good unusual fruit

Longan These are similar to lychees, but slightly more frost tolerant.

Loquat These are one of the first spring fruits, and taste like slightly tough apricots. They grow from seed, but grafted ones bear larger and earlier fruit. They are cold, drought and heat tolerant.

Lychee This grows in much the same conditions as avocados: it tolerates light frosts, but needs fertile, moist soil.

Nashi pear	This pear, with the crispness and shape of an apple, has a greenish-yellow skin and was developed in Japan. It should be allowed to ripen on the tree and is best eaten fresh, although it will store for at least three months. This 20th-century pear can be grown in cold, temperate or hot areas.
Peacharine	These are a cross between a peach and a nectarine, with large, smooth skinned fruit, yellow flesh and red-yellow skin. They will grow wherever peaches grow.
Persimmon	One of the most ornamental fruit trees, this small, rounded, and perfectly shaped tree has orange globes hanging from the branches in winter, after the leaves have turned red and fallen. Old-fashioned varieties were tart and seedy; newer ones are sweet and can be seedless. Persimmon can be grown from seed, but buy a grafted variety if you can.
Pineapple guava, or feijoa	This will grow in all but very cold areas. It is a small tree with green-red, tinged fruit which can be eaten fresh or processed.
Plumcott	This cross between a plum and an apricot, has apricot sized fruit with a flavour somewhere between the two. Plumcotts are slightly more frost resistant and drought hardy than apricots. Fruit fly don't seem to like them.
Sour cherry	This is quite different from the sweet cherry, *Prunus avium*. Sour cherry only grows to about two metres, whilst sweet cherry can reach twenty metres. It has dark, juicy, sour fruit, which can be used for jam or maraschino liqueur. It grows from seed or suckers, is extremely frost and drought resistant, and hardy: a good tree for small gardens.
Strawberry guava	The strawberry guava is frost sensitive. It grows about 6 metres tall, with white flowers and rich-flavoured red fruit of about 6 cm long. Eat them fresh, stewed or in jam.
White sapote	These are fast growing and cold tolerant (up to 5 degrees of frost). The yellow globe fruits are sweet and good.

Fruit the first year

- banana passionfruit
- berries
- cape gooseberries
- dwarf trees (many will bear in the first year of planting, especially nectarines and peaches)
- limes and lemons (most are sold at fruit-bearing size)
- melons
- mountain pawpaw
- passionfruit
- pawpaw
- pepino
- rhubarb
- tamarillo
- tomatillo

Edible fences

These can be heavily pruned and planted closely to make a thick hedge.

- avocado
- climbing fruits: kiwi fruit, black and banana passionfruit, hops, loganberries, marionberries, grapes
- dwarf trees, like apples, nectarines, peaches
- espaliered standard peaches, pears, apples
- feijoa
- hazelnuts
- kumquat
- limes

Fruit for cold areas

This list assumes that you'll:
- Try 'warmer' varieties against north-facing walls or in north-facing groves of other, sheltering trees.
- Choose late flowering varieties – many fruit trees are not killed by winter cold but by late frosts, after they've started to grow in spring.
- Start melons in cloches or greenhouses.

- babaco
- cape gooseberry
- citron
- dwarf peaches and nectarines
- feijoa
- figs
- kumquats
- limes
- mountain pawpaw
- pepino
- tamarillo

You can also try trees in tubs that can be brought inside.

Hardy fruiters

- apples – late flowering varieties
- banana passionfruit – against north-facing walls
- berries – strawberry, raspberry, brambleberries, gooseberry, cranberry
- Black cherry (*Prunus littoralis*)
- bunchberry
- cherries
- chestnut – warm slopes
- Chilean nut
- citron – north-facing slopes or warm walls
- citronelle or wild lemon – north-facing slopes or warm walls
- currants – red, black and white
- figs – north-facing slopes
- grapes – cold climate ones on north-facing slopes or against warm walls
- hazelnut
- Japanese raisin tree
- juniper
- kiwi fruit – keep it tall, against north-facing wall, and protect in first winter and spring
- linden
- loquat
- medlar
- mulberry – black, red and white
- olives – north-facing slopes
- peach – espaliered against a north wall
- pear
- persimmon
- pine nuts
- plum – late flowering varieties
- pomegranate – north-facing slope
- quince
- sloe
- walnut – warm north-facing slope

Temperate fruits

- almonds
- apples – late flowers
- apricot
- avocado
- babaco
- banana (warmer areas only – coastal and hot valleys)
- banana passionfruit – against north-facing walls
- berries – strawberry, raspberry, brambleberries, blueberries, cape gooseberry, gooseberry, cranberries
- bunya nut
- black sapote – like a chocolaty persimmon, warm areas only
- Brazil cherry
- carob
- cherries
- chestnut – warm slopes
- Chilean nut
- chinotto
- citron
- citronelle
- currants – red, black and white

- custard apples – warm north-facing slopes or walls
- feijoa
- figs
- ginko nuts
- grapefruit
- grapes
- hazelnut
- jakfruit (warm areas only)
- Japanese raisin tree
- juniper
- kei apple
- kiwi fruit
- lemon
- lime
- linden
- loquat
- lychee (wherever you grow avodados or citrus without protection)
- macadamia
- mountain pawpaw
- mulberry – black, red and white
- nashi pears
- natal plum
- nectarine
- olives
- orange
- passionfruit
- pawpaw (warm areas only)
- peach
- peacharine
- pear
- pecan
- persimmon
- pineapple (warm areas only)
- pine nuts
- pistachio
- plum
- plumcott
- pomegranate
- medlar
- nectarine
- quandong
- quince
- strawberry guava
- tamarillo – red, orange and golden
- walnut – warm north-facing slopes

Hot climate fruits

- acerloa cherry
- apples – some winter chilling needed
- apricot – some winter chilling needed
- avocado
- babaco
- bananas
- berries – strawberry, brambleberries, cape gooseberry
- bread fruit
- bunya nut
- black sapote
- Brazil cherry
- carob
- cashew nut
- Chilean nut
- coconut
- citronelle
- custard apples
- dates
- durian
- figs
- ginko nuts
- grapes – hot climate varieties only
- grumichama
- guava
- jakfruit
- Japanese raisin tree
- kaffir plum
- kiwi fruit (cooler areas only)
- lemon
- lime
- linden
- longan
- loquat
- lychee (wherever you grow avocados or citrus without protection)
- macadamia
- mango
- mangosteen
- mulberry – black, red and white
- natal plum
- orange
- passionfruit
- pawpaw
- peach (cool winters or with artificial chilling)
- pecan
- persimmon
- pineapple
- pine nuts
- plum (cool winters or with artificial chilling)
- quandong

- quince (cool winters or with artificial chilling)
- rosella
- sapodilla
- soursop
- star apple
- tamarind
- tamarillo – red, orange and golden
- walnut (cool winters or with artificial chilling)

Chapter 5

Growing in adversity

I live on an orchard in a valley near Braidwood, in southern New South Wales. The first few years I lived here were wonderful: a rich fresh creek, days of sun, and nights of rain. Then the drought came. The creek became a puddle guarded by wild ducks and dying wombats. The lettuce died in the heat, even with the drippers on them. And the young kiwi fruit vines shrivelled, although I kept the soil damp.

I began to learn how to grow things during the hard times.

Most Australians never know times like that: even in droughts the garden hose protects them – as does the knowledge that the supermarket will always provide. I prefer to live in contact with the world around me – too much insulation cuts off half your life.

Even with an ever-generous hose and a nearby supermarket, it is a good idea to learn how to grow things with very little water. Most of Australia is short of water – your tap water is probably pumped to you at enormous cost, both in terms of money and its ecological impact. A lot of domestic water is high in salts, chlorine and fluoride – which can all build up in the soil and are bad for growing things.

Too little water can kill plants, or stunt them. But sometimes mild water stress is good for your garden. Plants are encouraged to send their roots deeper down, becoming more drought tolerant; soft, disease-prone growth is reduced; and plants can be gradually 'hardened off' to the lack of water. When fruit is ripening, too much water can split it. Mild water stress, for example when flower buds are forming on many fruit trees, will increase the number of buds, though this shouldn't continue once the buds start to develop. Less water while fruit is growing usually means smaller fruit – but the fruit may also have a better flavour, improved keeping qualities, and excellent texture.

Wherever water is scarce or expensive, the aim of any gardener is to use as little as possible without causing water stress.

How to use less water

1 Water only when needed. Don't water just because it's Tuesday, and you always water the garden on Tuesdays. Stick your finger in the soil. Surface dryness is no indication of dry soil – just as a moist surface doesn't mean there's moisture below.
2 Water only as deep as the roots.
3 Mulch. Any mulch – even stones and newspaper – is better than nothing.
4 Time your watering. Try watering in the evening or, if you are worried about powdery mildew on damp foliage, in the early morning.
   Contrary to much gardening advice, one good watering a week may not be best for your garden. Plants do best with a constant water supply – not a weekly waterlogging. Give as much water as is needed to penetrate to the roots, and water again just before the plants start to wilt. To judge this is an art, but one soon learned by any person who closely watches their garden.
5 In hot areas, plant crops in the shade of pergolas or high vegetables like corn or lemon grass.
6 Use drip irrigation – you'll use perhaps one-tenth of the water you use now, with better results.
7 Plant drought tolerant native species or perennials whenever possible – the longer a plant lives the bigger its root system gets, and the more drought proof it becomes.

Trench gardens

An ancient method of growing vegetables in areas where there is not much moisture is trench gardening.

Dig a trench, as long as you like, but no more than one metre wide or you won't be able to reach across it. Angle it east-west, so it catches the sunlight. Let it slope slightly, so moisture doesn't just sit in the one spot, but runs down the trench. Slope the sides to catch any rain or dew – any moisture. You can either leave the slopes bare or – better still – line them with plastic. Weigh the plastic down with rocks, cover with a second layer of plastic and secure with more rocks at the edges. At night, the moisture in the air between the layers will condense and seep down into the garden.

Now, either line it with a couple of centimetres of compost, or slightly disturb the surface. Plant your vegetables, and mulch well.

Don't bother with a sprinkler: on a hot day, up to 90 per cent of the water will be lost to evaporation. Just stick the end of the hose under the mulch at the uphill end of the trench, or at several points along it if it's long. If you think your trench doesn't slope, trickle water down it and see – nearly all

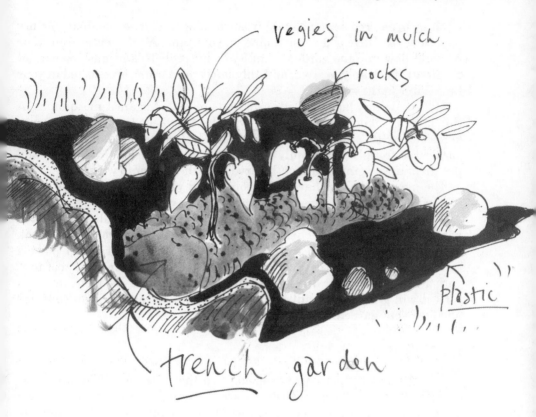

vegies in mulch.

rocks

plastic

trench garden

ground slopes somewhat, it may just be too slight a gradient to be easily visible.

This method can also be used to plant trees in dry areas: plant the trees in a slight hollow, then slope down the two layers of plastic. The longer the plastic, the more water will condense.

Collecting your own water

Every house should have a water tank. Not only does this give you reasonably pure water, it also lessens your contribution to the enormous areas that need to be flooded to keep our city lawns green. It's easy to forget the ecological cost of water when it flows out of your tap at a twist of the wrist. It is with water as it is with food and power and other services: if you have to help provide them yourself, you begin to realise how much you use of all of them – and the impact that has on the world around you.

Many councils forbid tanks in suburban areas. They are supposed to look ugly. Start lobbying and promise to grow jasmine over your tank to keep it scenic.

Many urban roofs are polluted from car and aeroplane exhausts, factory pollution, etc. Have a 'diversion pipe' on your tank. All the water from your roof will flow into the garden – until you divert it. This means you can let the first rain clean your roof, and only fairly pure water is collected in your tank, later in the storm.

Make sure any holes in your tank top are netted against mosquitoes. A thin layer of oil on top of the water will also help keep them out. Don't use kerosene, as that will hurt you too. As a last resort, install a filter – or gather the froth-like dragonfly eggs from a dam or creek or fishpond, and put them in your tank: dragonfly larvae kill the mosquito wrigglers.

The more tanks you have, the more water you can store: even a small roof will fill a twenty-thousand gallon tank many times a year over most of Australia. (During our last drought, our two-thousand gallon tank was kept topped up just by the heavy dews trickling down the roof into the tank at night.) Consider putting a tank next to your shed or garage; or place a tank next to the vegie garden and channel the water from your roof to it with a long length of drain pipe. If you throw weeds, seaweed, etc. into this tank it will give you instant liquid fertiliser whenever you want to water and feed your garden.

Cisterns

Tanks are usually placed high enough so the water can flow into your kitchen or into the garden. Cisterns are in-ground tanks and, unless they are on a hill above your house, you will need a pump to get the water up. But they do save space, and are less conspicuous than an above-ground tank.

'Grey' water

This is all your waste water, except for that from the toilet. It may be contaminated – small amounts of blood or faecal matter can be washed down showers or from the laundry – and waste water can be high in salt, soap, and detergents. Use it sparingly on trees and lawns, but not on your vegetables.

Frost

How many times have you heard someone say, 'I can't grow that, the frost will kill it.'

Frost is a bogeyman. It frightens people from growing a lot of things that might flourish with a bit of care. But the bogeyman can be controlled.

Remember that it isn't the frost itself that kills your plants: it's the thawing afterwards, as the swollen cells burst. You therefore have two options with frost: you can protect your garden from it, or you can make sure the thawing is gentle, and save your plants that way.

Avoiding frost

Look for frost-free sites

Learn to judge the frost potential of your garden. Even in a small area frost damage can vary enormously. Imagine frost as a body of cold air flowing like water. It will settle in hollows, flow down drains and air channels, and be easily blocked by fences, hedges and other plants. If frost can drain away it may leave the higher spots in your garden clear – especially if they are the warmer, north-facing spots.

My garden is on a slight slope with a ridge behind it. There are enough differences in micro-climate for me to grow raspberries and sugar maples in one part of my garden – where the sun is blocked till late morning and the frost stays till midday – and have avocados ripening within metres, where the frost drains away down a sunnier slope.

Watch how the frost settles in your garden before you do major plantings. Work out how your intended garden design might change the frost pattern: a new fence, for example, might block the frost and burn off plants previously untouched, whilst clearing a hedge could let frost drain away, or the slow growth of a large tree may gradually protect the plants beneath it.

Increase your frost-free area

Clear away any blockages if you can: weed piles and fences – or at least any long grass or bracken round the fences – so that frost can drain away. If you have a hedge or other shrubbery which you don't want to remove, try cutting low drainage holes in it.

Mulch

Mulch can help prevent roots from freezing. Dark mulches absorb heat during the day; mulches that trap moist air, like loosely packed hay, are also good – dark semi-rotted hay is ideal.

On the debit side, *a mulched or dug garden attracts more frost than one with a leafy covering of plants* – either clover or other vegetables. So, mulched plants may get their leaves frosted unless you put a plastic or hessian guard around them.

Plant thickly for winter – crowded gardens and orchards are much less frost prone – and make sure you have a living soil cover.

Snow

Snow will act as an insulator, and do less harm than frost. Don't clear it away from your garden – heap it up instead.

Seaweed and nettle tea spray

A weekly spray of seaweed or nettle tea is said to increase plants' resistance to frost and to help fruit set in cold areas. Both can be home-made: just cover seaweed or nettles with water, leave for a few weeks, and dilute to the colour of weak tea.

Irrigation

Overhead irrigation releases the latent heat of the water during spraying. For this to effectively help your crops you must start spraying when the temperature is still at least 2°C or more. You don't necessarily need large-scale commercial equipment for this: a garden spray or even microjets also work well.

Wind machines

These are used commercially to mix cold air with the warmer air above it. These machines can be bought or made at home. A ten horsepower motor driving a propeller on a ten metre tower is claimed to raise the temperature over one hectare by 2°C in a few minutes.

Predicting frost

Some gardeners swear they can smell a frost: a clear, sharp smell. It is the smell of cold, dry air. Frost is less likely when the sky is cloudy, or when there is a fog or other moisture around. Frosts can often be predicted by gazing at the sky at night. If the stars are particularly bright and twinkling there will probably be a frost.

Lighting fires around the garden is an old-fashioned way to keep off frost. The smoke from the fires is actually more useful than the heat from the flames. Orchardists used to use specially designed braziers that burnt all night with a lot of smoke. Cover a good bed of coals with green wood for a smoky fire. (This is not a remedy for suburban areas.)

Keep frost records from year to year. The dates of the first and last frost each year should be fairly consistent, though it can vary by up to a month or even more. It is helpful to know, for example, that last year your first frost came in late April and your last at the end of September. It is also a good reminder that, no matter how warm the air feels, last year a frost did come and wiped out your tomatoes.

Some frost prevention gardens

A high-mulched garden

Surround your garden with wire mesh or tomato stakes with string around them. Fill this circle with dry leaves or lightly packed hay, so only the tops of the plants show through. The mesh should stop the leaves from blowing away. Harvest crops through the mulch. Plants can dry out under this sort of mulch, and eventually they can rot. So, only leave the garden covered during the most dangerous frost times: about six weeks in late autumn or in early spring, for late harvesting or hardening off early plants.

Water in the garden

A pond in the middle of your garden will keep the area around it slightly warmer through the night. Keep your swimming pool full in winter and use it as heat storage for frost sensitive plants around it. Anyone who has watched steam rising from a lake or river in the early morning sees how bodies of water act as heat sinks.

The sheltered garden

Orange groves in England used to be planted in specially designed groves of other trees, tall and thick, that kept them sheltered. Use larger trees to protect smaller shrubs below.

Gardening out of frost's reach

Get some old tyres from the local garage and pile them high – as high as necessary to get your plants out of reach of the frost. If this means a pile of more than three tyres, drive a stake down the middle so they don't fall over. Now fill them with earth, compost, old hay or manure, preferably still decomposing: the decomposition will give a bit of added warmth, though it isn't essential. Plant your crops up top. Even fruit trees work with this method, as long as the whole thing is well-staked while the roots grow down below the level of the tyres. Water well though: drainage can be too good in tyre gardens.

You can of course build up your above-ground frost-free garden from other materials than old tyres – but tyres are easy to come by and, being thick and black, they absorb and retain heat well.

The flooded garden

An emergency method of keeping frost from your crops is to flood them. This is easy in a garden with waterproof (that is, concrete or mortared stone) permanent edges. Otherwise, edge the garden with boards, making sure the ends abut firmly.

Now line the garden with newspaper, at least 6 pages thick, making sure that the pages overlap and rise up to the top of the boards. Just before you go to bed, on any clear, starry night that smells of frost, fill the lined garden bed with water. Make it as deep as possible, and leave the hose just dripping into it. Take the boards away in the morning to drain away the water.

As long as you drain the water off in the morning you can use this method even with plants that are susceptible to collar rot, especially if you give them their own collars of newspaper to stop soil-borne spores from infecting them.

The manure-heated pit garden

Dig a hole about 60 cm deep and pile in leaves or still-decomposing manure. Cover with sandy soil. Plant your vegetables. Now lay a few stakes over the pit and cover it with clear plastic or old windows, balanced on a few bricks so that they are oriented to the morning sun.

The heat generated by the decomposing material should mean that the pit under the cold frame is relatively frost free. These beds can also be used to help strike cuttings which need bottom heat, or to obtain early seedlings for spring planting.

Heated frost frame

Make a manure or compost pile about 60 cm high. Lightly cover it with soil. Carefully fit a cold frame over the top of it, so the top is level with the top of the pile and the main slope is oriented to the morning sun. A good mix for the compost pile is equal parts of coarse leaves (not gum leaves) and fresh cow or horse manure. This mixture produces a good, long-lasting heat – but do experiment with any compostable material on hand.

Wait about a week before planting out the cold frame, to give the bed a chance to warm up evenly.

Repairing frost damage

The worst frost damage occurs when plants thaw rapidly. It is not so much the freezing that injures the plants as the thawing, when the frozen cells expand and burst. If you are an early riser give your plants a thorough, gentle watering before the sun hits them. This way the plant cells gradually relax instead of bursting. Even totally frozen plants can be restored this way.

Also try covering your plants to increase the thawing time – do this either in the evening, or race out and do it as soon as you see frost on the ground. Use anything – blankets, old newspaper – just get your plants covered. This may often save them.

As a last resort rely on frost-hardy plants and ones that have been hardened to your area. Any plant bought from an area hotter than yours, or from an indoor area in a nursery, may well tolerate less frost than a local plant. You can harden plants gradually by leaving them outside for longer and longer periods each day. Better still, raise your own from cuttings or seed taken from plants which grow happily in your area.

Speeding up crops in cold areas

1 Protect your plants from the wind. You feel colder when a high wind is blowing – and plants suffer too. A windbreak (either trees or other plants or

– even better – a walled courtyard) might mean you can grow things in less time than anyone else around.

2 Add a greenhouse to the side of your house, preferably the kitchen, so you can share the warmth. Make a temporary greenhouse out of a frame of semi-circular polypipe propping up plastic, weighted down by stones or held in the soil with stakes.

3 Try old windows propped up on bricks over your plants, or miniature green houses (plastic bottles with the bottoms cut out).

4 Mulch with a heat-absorbing and reflecting mulch, like stones.

5 Use a seaweed spray: it appears to increase frost resistance and root growth, which makes plants hardier.

6 Add potash to your plants in early autumn, for hardier new growth. Avoid high-nitrogen fertilisers that promote soft, sappy growth.

7 A new, commercial, woven plant cover helps new spring growth enormously, and gives some frost protection.

Chapter 6

Scavenging
the suburbs

Many of the street trees in your area are probably useful – as are a lot of your common garden weeds, and many of your flowers. In fact, very few ornamentals didn't have some use, traditionally – our ancestors were canny with their gardens, and either planted useful species or found a use for the others. Avoid harvests near highways and busy streets though, as they may be high in lead.

Street trees

Hibiscus

Make hibiscus tea by pouring boiling water onto the flowers – it is slightly laxative and delicious, perhaps my favourite. You can also eat the flowers stuffed with rice etc., and simmered in stock, or deep-fried in batter.

Pickle the buds in spiced vinegar – just pour over boiling vinegar with brown sugar or honey to taste, and a touch of cloves and mixed spice. Eat them after six weeksm, like olives.

Young hibiscus shoots and buds can be eaten raw in salads or boiled as a vegetable; or steam them and serve them cold with vinaigrette dressing.

Hibiscus fruit – the seed container that matures after the petals drop off – can be eaten fresh or cooked.

Horse chestnuts

These are often planted as street trees in cooler areas. Cut the chestnuts into slices, cover with water and change every day till it doesn't taste bitter. Place the slices on aluminium foil to dry, outside or in a cool oven. Grind them to flour when they are crisp. Add this to cakes and biscuits for a richer flavour: one dessertspoon chestnut flour to one cupful ordinary flour. I make horse-chestnut pancakes with one dessertspoon ordinary flour to one cupful of chestnut flour. 'Red' chestnuts – or any nuts for that matter – also make good 'flour'.

collecting acorns

Irish strawberry tree

The fruit is edible – sometimes good enough to eat fresh, sometimes better stewed with sugar. It also makes excellent chutney. Like most ornamentals, strawberry trees haven't been selected for their ability to give good fruit: some are much better than others, and worth hunting down.

Kurrajongs

Eat the fruit – some are better than others. The roots are edible too – you can cook them like parsnips – and a small harvest won't hurt the tree. But you may feel conspicuous digging up roots on the footpath.

Oak trees

Acorns can be used to make flour, oil or coffee. Taste them – if they are bitter, soak them in water until they taste sweet. Make acorn oil by drying the acorns for a week in the sun; cracking them with a hammer, then weighing them in a sieve with a weight on top; let the oil seep out over at least one week.

To make acorn flour, dry the acorns in the oven till crisp – this may take between five and six hours. Crack them with a hammer, then grind in the blender. Acorn flour is very rich, and can be used in the same way as horse-chestnut flour.

Fried acorns

Take sweet, soaked acorns; soak them again overnight in a cup of water with one dessertspoon of honey; deep-fry them in hot oil until they float to the surface. Eat them hot, with a sprinkle of salt if that's what you like with peanuts, for example.

Palms

The sap of many palms is sweet – drill a small hole, and find out. Most saps need to be boiled to reduce them to make them sweet enough for cooking or on pancakes.

Paperbark

Paperbark trees are a common street tree in Sydney. Use the paper-like bark as insulation under your carpet or in the roof; or glue some sheets together to make a waterproof blanket over a child's mattress.

Pines

Many pines – not just stone pines and Swiss pines – produce edible nuts, though many are too small to be worth extracting commercially. Taste them and see.

Wattle

Some wattle seeds are edible – ignore them if they're bitter. Layer wattle blossom in sugar or pale honey, and use it as a flavouring instead of vanilla. Taste wattle gum – it flows readily in summer. If it's bitter leave it alone, unless you want a cure for constipation – otherwise melt it in hot water and add fruit juice or cordial; then let it set like jelly. *Acacia farnesia* seeds are supposed to be an aphrodisiac – I've tried them on friends, chooks and a Indian game rooster, without noticeable effects.

Using weeds

A few years ago I went to a market in Granada in Spain. There were Gypsies and farmers with bundles and baskets, colour and laughter and haggling. Housewives weighed and sorted, old men considered. We shouldered through the crowd, hoping for green piles of artichokes or purple mounds of eggplant. There on the tables were bunches of drab, dusty, quite unmistakable ... weeds: in Granada, Thursday is weed market.

Most gardeners complain about weeds. No-one ever complains about having too many carrots. Yet, like weeds, carrots go to seed and spread through bare ground, through the lawn, into pots of geraniums ... the difference is that everyone knows what to do with carrots. We've lost our skill with weeds.

One hundred years ago weeds were used, even in Australia. Cottagers made wine with them; stewed them up for dinner; drank them medicinally, or made healing salves for scratches. Now, few gardeners grow anything they haven't already seen packaged in supermarkets. We look at 'bush tucker' on the telly, but forget about the wild harvests in our own backyards.

Not all weeds are edible. All, however, have some use: our ancestors were too thrifty to let any wild crop go unharvested. The following suggestions are just a few of the things you can do with weeds.

Eating weeds

Spring is the best time to eat weeds. Most are tough and bitter during summer. Choose young shoots, preferably after rain, and eat them in salads: dandelions, sow thistles, sorrel, blackberry, a few oxalis leaves, very young cobbler's pegs, burdock, young wandering jew shoots, dock leaves, chicory, or bracken. Bitter, older leaves can be steamed or boiled – even more bitter ones can be simmered in milk.

Roots can be good, too. Scrape burdock root clean and bake it in cider. Bracken roots are excellent if you get young ones. Oxalis ceases to be a problem once you find its bulblets are better than any water chestnut: serve them stir-fried, or added to stews for crunch.

Many people know about dandelion coffee. Dig up a dandelion root – the older the better, but winter roots are sweetest. Clean it, place it in the oven until it is dry and brittle, and grind it in a flour mill or blender – if it won't grind, it needs more drying. Mix one tablespoon with a cup of water or milk in a saucepan, bring this to the boil and, if necessary, let it stand so the grains fall to the bottom. Dandelion coffee is reputed to stimulate the appetite, and to be a digestive and anti-rheumatic, an excellent tonic, and a very mild laxative.

Dandelion roots are good eaten like parsnips. Scrub them well, peel them if you can, lay them in a baking dish, cover with cider and dot with butter. Bake until they are tender and the cider is a lovely, rich gravy. Serve hot. You can also steam or boil them and mash them with plenty of butter.

Even couch grass roots can be cleaned and steamed, or chopped and stir-fried with other vegetables – if you can be bothered. A steady diet of couch grass roots might harm your health – but the occasional taste does no harm. I have tried them steamed, then dipped in soy sauce and sesame oil, which makes anything taste good. Never eat raw couch grass roots – they must be well cooked.

Many weeds' seeds are also good. The oily seeds of pigweed can be ground to meal and baked like a biscuit or added to stews to thicken them; the stems and leaves can be boiled or eaten fresh in salads, though they taste a bit slimy if uncooked. They are good pickled or crystalised in a strong sugar or honey solution.

Try fried thistly buds – after all, artichokes are really only a superior thistle. Take very young sow thistle buds; scrape off the prickles, if any – if there are a lot the buds are too old. Dip them in a batter of plain flour mixed with beaten egg and deep-fry them in hot oil until they're light brown and just rising to the surface. If the buds are large, they are too old to fry. Eat them hot, with a little natural yoghurt and garlic.

Drinking weeds

These are the classic cottager drinks – cheap and simple and refreshing.

Nettle beer
1 kilo nettle leaves
2 lemons
1 tablespoon cream of tartar
4 litres water
500 g brown sugar
1 teaspoon dried yeast
This used to be a popular country beer, reputed to be good against rheumatic ailments or depression – well, that was as good a reason as any for drinking it!

Boil the nettles and water for a quarter of an hour; strain; add the sugar, pith of the fruit (no white), strained juice and cream of tartar. Stir; add the yeast when lukewarm. Cover and leave for three days. Strain out all sediment and bottle. Use after a week to ten days.

This is a strongly fermenting beer – don't keep it too long, or the bottle may burst.

Horehound beer
Boil a cup of chopped horehound leaves in 6 litres of water with 50 g of treacle. Strain, cool, add a teaspoon of dried yeast when it's lukewarm. Cover with a clean tea-towel. Bottle after 24 hours. Check the bottles every day and release the pressure or they may burst. Drink after three days in warm weather, about a week in cool weather.

Couch grass beer
This is supposed to be a kidney tonic.

Pull up your couch grass, roots and all. Wash it well – grit neither adds to the flavour nor to the supposed medicinal qualities. For every three cups of couch add 4 litres of water, 4 cups of sugar, two sliced lemons and two sliced oranges (with their skin on). Boil until the skins are tender and mashable; strain; add a teaspoon of dried yeast when lukewarm. Cover with a tea-towel; bottle after three days; check every day to make sure the bottles won't explode, and drink after a week.

Oxalis tonic wine

This isn't a wine, and for all I know it isn't a tonic either. It has the same bitter quality as stout, which is also supposed to be a strengthener and blood purifier – or so said my Irish grandfather, 'Ah, you can feel it doing you good!' I can imagine oxalis tonic wine being doled out by the tablespoonful to ungrateful children – but then I don't like stout either.

Take a cup of chopped oxalis leaves, boil in 4 litres of water for 10 minutes, then strain. Pour into a bucket with 500 g of brown sugar and a teaspoon of cream of tartar; stir till the sugar is dissolved. Add a teaspoon of dried yeast when it's lukewarm; cover with two tea-towels and leave in a warm room for three days. Strain out the sediment; bottle in screw-topped bottles. Store the bottles on their sides. The beer is ready in two weeks. It doesn't keep well: put it in the fridge as soon as it's drinkable, and don't keep it for more than a week.

Dandelion wine

Boil for one hour: 2 litres of dandelion flowers in 4 litres of water with the rinds of two oranges and two lemons and 1.25 kg of sugar. Cool till tepid; add the juice of the oranges and lemons, 50 g of raisins and two tablespoons of fresh yeast or its dried equivalent.

Leave for 24 hours; strain and bottle without screwing down the tops. Do this only when fermentation has finished – which may be after a month or more.

Medicinal weeds

How many people remember the old horehound lollies for a cough? Horehound (*Marrubium vulgare*) grows to one metre, a bushy perennial with rounded, grey, furry, soft leaves and white flowers. Pour boiling water on the leaves for a cough syrup; candy the stems for cough lollies, or add the horehound tea to toffee. I make horehound lollies with a cup of horehound stems (peel them if they are old and tough) to a cup of honey. Boil rapidly till a little sets in a saucer of cold water – after about ten to fifteen minutes. Place the candies on a board or greaseproof paper until they've set, then wrap them individually in greaseproof paper and store them in a sealed jar. Give them to children to suck.

Boiled dock leaves can be used as a poultice on wounds and sprains. There is some debate about whether these are more effective hot, or cold from the freezer – I incline to the latter. Stewed leaves can be used as a tonic for liver complaints.

Even cobbler's pegs (*Bidens pilosa*) have their medicinal uses. Cobbler's pegs are the narrow spined fruit that stick to you when you brush past them. They're called farmer's friends round where I live – because they stick to you, and stick to you, and stick to you. Make an infusion of cobbler's pegs flowerheads against diarrhoea and coughs. The flowers can be chewed against toothache.

Dill (*Anethum graveolens*) is a common weed round Sydney and other temperate parts of Australia, often growing beside the road or in waste areas. It is a tall, feathery, dark green plant that smells of anise. It is easily confused with fennel – not surprisingly, as they can hybridise. Drink dill tea as a digestive; give it to babies for colic; feed it to lactating mothers – human or animal – to increase milk yield.

For a simple cradle cap remedy, bring a cup of chickweed almost to the boil in olive oil. Take off the heat, cool, and strain. Rub the oil gently onto the scalp, then wash off with warm soapy water.

Eating flowers

Most flowers taste as good as they smell. Roses are one of the best. Cut out the white base of each petal, as they're bitter. Scatter them in salads; marinate them in oil or vinegar for their taste and perfume; roll them around marzipan and slice for multicoloured sweets.

Use dianthus or carnations instead of cloves; scatter chrysanthemum petals for a smoky bitter taste in salads – a bit like rocket.

Stuff gladioli flowers, or zucchini or pumpkin flowers with leftover fried rice – or slip them in batter and fry. Use violets in custards or creams for natural sweetening; try violas or primulas in salads or sandwiches; use a few borage flowers for a cucumber flavour, or pelargonium flowers for edible decoration. The leaves can also be used as flavouring – dipped in custard and removed after cooking, like you'd use a bay leaf.

Citrus flowers make a lovely jam – and are good in salads too. So are chopped chive flowers, whilst elderflowers make a good 'champagne'.

Elderflower champagne
This should need no yeast, except for the natural yeast on the flowers. If it doesn't begin to ferment in four warm days though, add a pinch of dried yeast.
8 young elderflower heads (not old ones – they smell like where the cat has been)
1 kg white or raw sugar
half a cup of white wine vinegar
3 large sliced lemons or 6 sliced limes

Remove petals from the elderflowers. Mix all ingredients in a large bowl. Cover with a clean tea-towel. Leave for three days. Add a little yeast if there are no bubbles. Leave another 24 hours. Strain. Bottle. Leave for one to three months before drinking. Release pressure often.

Chapter 7

Small animals for small gardens

All peasant cultures keep animals – not necessarily big animals, but little ones that eat the scraps and help provide protein and manure. Crop yields from areas that have had animals grazing on them are always higher than the nutrient input would suggest, partly because of the bacterial and other activity created in the soil.

All natural ecosystems contain animals. If yours doesn't have any, you just have to imitate their function: by cutting grass yourself instead of letting them eat it, composting scraps and weeds and debris instead of letting chooks or goats turn it into manure.

The cheapest way I know of feeding your plants is to buy animal food, like wheat or laying pellets or hay, and feeding it to small animals – then using the dung from those animals to feed your crops.

There is an old English saying, which explains how the Romney marshes got to be fertile: 'To be able to graze twelve sheep to the acre, you graze twelve sheep to the acre till it can.' In other words, keep bringing in food for the animals until the fertility accumulates to feed them without further additions.

Animals can also be used to keep weeds down: goats like blackberry, and guinea pigs, hens and rabbits can be placed in cages over weeds; or this can be done to prepare an area for planting.

There's another reason to keep animals, too. Once humans shared the world with other species. Now we lock ourselves in cities, sterile places, where we're dominated by other human beings. I believe it makes life richer to share it with other species: the wild animals you can attract to share your world (even if they are only birds and lizards, or insects like bees or butterflies and hoverflies), and the other animals: pets and small domesticates, which will share your life.

Nobody owns land. Ownership just means that it doesn't belong to any other human. Animals don't recognise exclusive ownership of land by one

species, nor have we any right to impose it on them.

Even a small backyard is inhabited by literally tens of thousands of creatures. Most are too small to be seen or noticed: insects, parasites on insects, etc. Others, like birds, are welcome sharers. Maximise your diversity:

- avoid pesticides, herbicides and fungicides which kill non-target organisms;
- grow as many diverse species as you can (especially flowering shrubs and vegetables gone to seed – for blossom feeders and the creatures which eat the blossom eaters);
- have tall trees and low cover;
- provide water baths for birds and insects;

- build stone or log walls for lizards and frogs . . .
- but most of all, use no pesticides – including in your house.

More pesticides are used in the home than in farms and gardens. Concentrate on growing things, not on killing things. Enjoy the world, don't add to its destruction.

Using manure

No manure should be used fresh – especially not bird manure. Bird manure also contains their urine, and may burn your crops. Leave it until it's dry. But you can use fresh manure to make liquid manure: just cover it with water, and use the water for your crops when it is the colour of weak tea – no stronger or it may burn the leaves or roots.

Make sure chook pens are kept dry to lessen fly problems. Wet manure stinks. Clean your outpens regularly and fill them with straw or other bedding (even weeds and grass clippings) that will soak up moisture.

The CSIRO has been studying the lesser mealworm beetle: it lives in manure, dries it out, and turns it into a powder that doesn't attract flies and can be used as a fertiliser. If you are interested, ask for the information leaflet at your nearest Government bookstore.

Never use human, pig, dog or cat manure – they all share too many parasites and diseases. If you wish to save the nutrients, throw them in a deep hole – at least 1.5 metres deep – and grow deep-rooted comfrey on top. Harvest the comfrey and use it as mulch. You can also bury such manure in deep trenches between fruit trees.

How to kill a bird for meat

Catch the bird at night when it's roosting, and place it in a small cage if you don't want to kill it at once. This means you don't have to chase it round in the morning when it's wide awake. It also means its guts will be empty, which makes cleaning a bit easier.

I usually chop the head off. It is messy, but quick. Place the head on a chopping block, chin down and eyes up, with the bird suspended above, its neck arched. This makes it hard for the bird to move. I hold the axe near the base – you can't swing it this way, but you don't need much force to kill a bird. Otherwise it's hard to use the axe and hold the bird at the same time, unless you have very long arms.

You could make a metal or hard cardboard cone, and force the head through this, to stop the wings flapping. This makes the job easier, but also terrorises the bird. If you are fast with the axe they won't realise what's happening.

An alternative is to hold the legs in one hand and the neck in the other, and pull. This breaks its neck. I've never quite had the courage to try this. You then need to cut the head off afterwards, to let the bird bleed. The blood used to be kept to thicken the gravy.

Now dump the bird in very hot water. Add detergent for a water bird like duck or goose to help the water penetrate. Leave the bird in the hot water till you can rub off the leg feathers – about 30 seconds. Now dump it in cold water (or run the cold tap over it) to stop it from cooking. Rub off the small feathers. If they won't rub off, put it back into the hot water again for a few seconds. Pluck out the large wing feathers. Put the feathers on wet newspaper to stop them from blowing away – and get into everything.

Cut off the feet. Wriggle your fingers under the neck skin to find the 'crop' – which will contain whatever the bird has been eating last. Pull it out. It will be like an irregularly stuffed balloon, and shouldn't break.

Now you need to gut the bird. Look for the vent, where the droppings come out. Get a sharp, pointed knife and cut around it: it's like a long tube. Be careful not to break it. When it is free, wriggle your hand in along one side of the bird and take all the organs in your hand. This sounds hard, but it isn't. Scoop them up and pull them out gently. Keep the heart, liver and gizzard (the red bits) and use them for stock with the neck and feet. If you're really keen, you can rinse out the 'tubes' for sausages or storing fat, etc.

Rinse the bird. Let it cool for a day to 'set' if you're going to roast, fry or barbecue it. For a casserole, the birds can be used straight away.

Using feathers

Feathers can be used to stuff pillows, quilts or even mattresses – though feather mattresses do turn lumpy quickly, unless you shake them every day. Unfortunately, feathers need to be 'dry plucked' to be used in quilts, or they lose their fluff. This takes forever. Should you decide you want the feathers enough to compensate for a long, slow job, pull out the fluffy leg and body feathers first. These are the ones you want. Then dunk the bird in hot water to pull out the long, tough feathers which need to be discarded anyway.

Feathers are high in nutrients and good for compost. But don't use them for mulch – they blow away.

Killing small animals

Small animals need to be skinned, not plucked. Hang them up by the hind legs, slit the skin, and start to pull it downwards, separating the skin from fat and membrane. This needs strength in both fingers and wrists, even for small animals like rabbits. The best rabbit skinner I've ever known was in her seventies and a fanatical knitter – she had muscles in her thumbs. Try not to let the outside of the skin touch the meat, in case it taints it.

After skinning, cut around the anus, then slit the animal down the belly – not too deep or you might puncture the innards. Gently ease out the guts, making sure they don't fall on your boots.

Young animals can be fried or grilled; older animals are best slowly baked, steamed, or boiled. Generally, the meat along the backbone is the most tender, and the hindlegs more tender than the forelegs. Butchering larger animals is a matter of practice. If you ask your butcher nicely they may let you watch them carve a beast or two, and it may be worthwhile paying a butcher to joint your first large beast so you can learn how to do it.

References

There are a lot of books on keeping (small) animals – check your local library first:

Australian Goat Husbandry, Pat Coleby, Night Owl Publishers, Shepparton 1985

Earthworms for Gardeners and Fishermen, Department of Agriculture, Victoria

A Guide to Keeping Bees in Australia, Norman Redpath, Viking O'Neil, Melbourne 1990

A Guide to Keeping Poultry in Australia, Dorothy Reading, Nelson, Melbourne 1981

The Fresh Water Aquaculture Book, William McLarney, Hartley & Marks, Vancouver 1984

The Healthy House Cow, Marja Fitzgerald, Earth Garden Books, Trentham 1989

In most States, the Department of Agriculture also publishes notes on animal husbandry, so they're well worth contacting too.

Bees

Advantages	Like birds, bees bring nutrients from elsewhere to your place. Don't underestimate the droppings of a million bees – or their honey or pollen. Bee pollen can also be rubbed on pest-prone plants to attract lacewings and hoverflies. You can attract wild bees with plenty of flowers.
Disadvantages	Bees need care, and some people are allergic to them.

Carpet snakes

Advantages	They turn rodents into dung.
Disadvantages	They can scare people off, though this may be an advantage, of course. They are also only for warm areas – they hibernate in the cold.

Cows

Advantages	Cows give milk, meat and manure. Dexter cows are small and said to be docile – they're the classic peasant house cow. They can be tethered, made into pets, and grazed on footpaths in semi-rural areas.
Disadvantages	They are big, and probably not suited to most urban settings.

Ducks

Advantages	They produce meat and eggs, and are good snail hunters, if trained to it and provided they've been given other green stuff to free-range on before being let into the garden. Ducks are very decorative and can become pets – which makes it hard to eat them.
Disadvantages	They will pollute any swimmable water nearby, and they must be protected from dogs, cats and foxes. Their droppings can be messy and attract flies. Ducks don't give as many eggs as hens: their taste is slightly stronger, and the whites are slightly tougher.

Earthworms

Advantages	Earthworm help organic matter decompose, they increase the availability of nutrients, and improve the texture of the soil. They will turn garbage into nutrients. Earthworms can also be eaten, but you probably won't want to.
	Catch them wild, answer an advertisement from any gardening magazine, or let your natural population build up by adding mulch to the soil.
Disadvantages	Earthworms aren't cuddly. They don't make good pets. Many bought varieties don't survive in the wild, and they need regular feeding and tending.

Geese

Advantages	Meat (wonderful) and eggs. They're excellent watch dogs, and can be hilarious to watch. They are great in orchards – they keep down the grass and weeds, and eat fallen fruit.
Disadvantages	Geese are noisy and messy. Their droppings are runny and attract flies; they may be too vigilant as watch dogs, and males may attack your best friends. Their raucous sex lives begin at 4 a.m. in the morning and continue at ten-minute intervals for three months. Geese also love company: fence them away from the house, or be prepared for messy verandahs.
	Geese need swimmable water, or at the very least water they can puddle in and duck their heads under. Give them a handful of wheat every night to keep them tame. They must have good grass: if you haven't got greenery all year round, don't keep geese.

Goats and sheep

Advantages	They produce hair, meat, milk, and concentrated fertility. They can be tethered where needed.
Disadvantages	They need informed care and are vulnerable to dogs. Both goats and sheep will eat the garden: fruit trees and anything else, given the chance. While goats and sheep can be tethered, they should be trained to do this young – and be given plenty of free-ranging as well. Prolonged confinement is bad for any animal – for humans too.

Goldfish and other fish

Advantages	Fish are wonderful concentrators of fertility – just scoop out dirty water and use it on the garden. They need less care than many other livestock. Even goldfish can be eaten, but you probably won't want to.
Disadvantages	Fish need a clean water source – and most cities' water supplies aren't clean any more.

Guinea pigs

Advantages	They are small, make good pets, and can be eaten. They are excellent weed controllers if moved round the garden in mobile pens, like hens. They can also be milked, but you probably won't bother.
Disadvantages	Guinea pigs are vulnerable to dogs and cats, and to heat and cold. They also escape easily.

Hens

Advantages	They produce eggs and meat, and are friendly presences. Chooks make good pets – bantams especially are good for kids. Hens in the orchard eat fallen fruit, spread nutrients, catch grasshoppers and act as general pest controllers. Organic wheat, and other grains to feed them, can be obtained relatively easily. Hens are good rubbish disposers, especially of fruit fly and pest-infected fruit generally. A backyard can probably support about 6 free-range chooks with kitchen and garden scraps – more if food is imported. Hens can be housed in mobile pens and moved round the garden to control weeds and spread fertility. They can also be used as ploughs: make a bottomless mobile pen and let them thoroughly scratch any area that needs to be dug. This can also be done on a wider scale. I have used chooks to scratch and weed a potato field.
Disadvantages	Hens must be protected from dogs and foxes. Neighbours dislike roosters – but roosters need not be kept. Hens will scratch up vegetables. But if you only let them into the garden after a day's free-ranging on other green stuff, they'll simply go for slugs and snails.

Peacocks, guinea fowl, pheasants

Advantages	These produce plenty of manure, and can be kept as status symbols or pets.

Disadvantages   They are noisy, scratch the garden, and produce few eggs. They usually go exactly where you don't want them – but you can't bear to get rid of them. It's probably best to avoid them, unless you are enthusiastic.

Rabbits

Advantages   Rabbits are small, and can be fed on kitchen and garden scraps. They breed quickly and are easily tamed. Like chooks, rabbits can be housed in small pens (but let them out often), and moved around the garden to control weeds and fertilise the soil.

Disadvantages   They are vulnerable to dogs, cats and too much food from kids. Their rapid breeding is a problem unless you want to eat them or keep them celibate. Rabbits can be lovable and you may find it hard to eat them once you've kept them.

Rats and mice

Advantages   Rats and mice are small, breed quickly, and will eat almost anything. They can be eaten, but you probably won't want to. Both the dung and corpses of rats and mice are good fertiliser. While not advocating you keep them for either product, they are worth considering if you happen to be looking for a pet.

Disadvantages   They are small, breed quickly, and will eat almost anything – and they can escape. Their cage needs to be cleaned often.

Turkeys

Advantages   Meat, eggs, and spreaders of fertiliser. Turkeys provide a good moral lesson on the disadvantages of too much dignity.

Disadvantages   More temperamental and disease-prone than other poultry, they also give fewer eggs. You need to know what you are doing with turkeys.

Wild birds

Advantages   Once your garden is set up to attract them, feeding them is free. Birds that perch and nest in your garden will bring in nutrients from elsewhere. This shouldn't be underestimated, as anyone who has kookaburras perching on the clothes line can tell you – wild birds are as good at producing dung as chooks, and they are excellent pest catchers.

Disadvantages   Birds may eat fruit, flowers, seeds and pet food.

Chapter 8

Keeping the surplus

Why bother keeping food when you can eat it fresh? At any time of year your garden should be producing more varieties than you ever bothered getting from the supermarket. Even as I write, in spring – traditionally the 'hungry gap' when winter's crops are finished and spring's are not yet ready –)we're eating well: asparagus whenever I can be bothered crossing the creek to the asparagus paddock, artichokes which come up by themselves each year, a dozen sorts of 'annual' vegetables – many of which re-seed themselves without any help from me – tamarillos and banana passionfruit, and four sorts of citrus, and late avocados and early strawberries, and the tiny potatoes that have grown through winter in black tyres (a red-bellied black snake overwintered in them too) . . . so why preserve?

Firstly, because we're used to eating many seasonal crops all year round – particularly tomatoes. What's pizza without tomato, or winter without a pizza? Secondly, because there's a limit to how many zucchinis you can press on friends – and it's even harder to consign them to the compost.

Thirdly, because its fun. There's something reassuring about groaning shelves of last season's produce. It satisfies something basic – an ancestral memory of sieges, perhaps.

And, of course, there are the times when it's raining and you don't want to splash down to the vegie garden or get raindrops down your back as you pick some apples . . . the times when it's dark and you're tired and you just want to haul something off the shelves.

Storing food

For several years I lived in a shed, with no fridge or electricity, no freezer and no shop nearby. I learnt how to store things the old-fashioned way – the methods that have worked for thousands of years: like packing the butter in a bottle suspended in the creek on days of over 46°C in the shade; keeping meat in wine for a fortnight (it was wonderful when I finally got

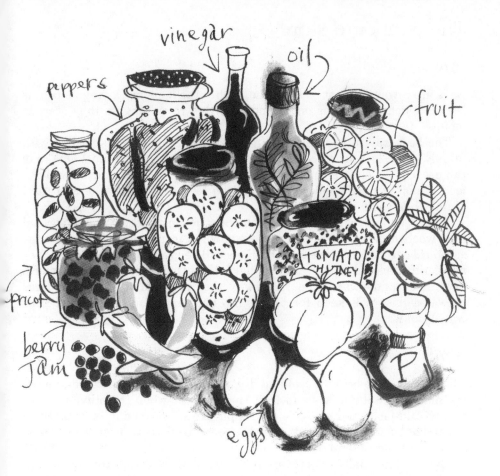

round to roasting it), or wrapping bottles of milk in wet tea-towels. I also learnt how to keep, from season to season, the produce I grew.

None of the methods were complicated: dried ears of corn stuffed in a box where the rats couldn't get at them (when I needed corn I scraped the kernels into soup or a stew); apricots dried on aluminium foil outside the shed (the wombat ate half of them and suffered for days), then packed in old coffee jars; pumpkins on the rafters; newspaper-wrapped apples; potatoes in hessian sacks in a dark, dry corner; eggs in cartons under the bed; and onions, garlic, and herbs hanging from the ceiling.

It's easy to store your surplus. It's harder to get rid of the supermarket assumption that all fruit and vegetables must be plump, glossy and perfectly packaged.

The cupboard store

Eggs

Eggs are always a feast or a famine. Either the hens are laying as fast as they can get their bums on the nest, or they're sulking as they start to moult.

The best way to keep eggs is in a rich fruit cake. Well splashed with brandy, these last for a year or more and get better all the time. One cake can use a dozen eggs. A couple of fruit cakes in the cupboard means you can feed a mob of bushwhalkers who happen to call in, or give one to Aunt Maud when you forget her birthday.

Eggs keep, untreated, for several months as long as their protective coat isn't washed off. Never wet eggs. Keep them in a cool, dark place – the standard egg cartons are excellent. Eggs will keep for a year or more if they are gently covered with a coat of clarified butter or candle wax, or of a mixture of candle wax and paraffin wax, then wrapped in newspaper. Eggs in water-glass will keep for two years, but first you have to find your water-glass.

Fruit

All fruit needs to be kept cool and dry, in an airy spot. Fruit produces the ripening agent ethylene – and fruit ripens faster when the ethylene can't escape. Old-fashioned methods of wrapping fruit in paper, or burying them in sand or bran were really designed to soak up ethylene as well as to keep the fruit cool, dark and dry.

Most commercial fruit is waxed. Waxed fruit rots from the inside out. Organically grown, unwaxed fruit just shrivels ... and shrivels ... and shrivels. After a few months it looks awful unless it's been in cool store – but the taste is often even better, and sweeter, than when the fruit was almost fresh. Straight from the tree, though, fruit is unbeatable: it still tastes of sunlight.

I once kept one of our untreated organic oranges for two years on a shelf. It had taken on an interesting, obscene shape. Then someone ate it. He said it was quite good – though by then the skin was dry and hard.

Healthy oranges keep a long time – the skins just get harder. Keeping them in the fridge slows down the mould – it doesn't help keep the oranges, which are best kept on a dry shelf where they can slowly desiccate.

Apples need to be kept cool – they will ripen as much in one day at 20°C as in ten days at 0°C. Try the fridge or dig a cool pit in a shady place, or store them in the best insulated part of the house. Try packing them in crumpled newspaper. This also keeps codling moth away. One friend took an old fridge and buried it, door upwards, in the shade and stored the apples there. To get to the apples you just open the door. (*Warning*: remove the catch on such an old fridge, so children can't get trapped in them.)

An old-fashioned way of storing grapes was to keep them unbroken in their bunch – having removed all bad ones – and to cover them gently with bran or sawdust, making sure that no grape touches any other. This is fiddly but effective: grapes will stay fresh in a cool place for months. The sawdust or bran method also works with other soft fruit, like apricots, firm-skinned peaches, plums, and pears as well as apples.

Vegetables

Don't keep vegies near fruit: the fruit's ethylene will make them rot faster. I keep most of our vegies on wire racks in a dark, airy cupboard. There are now commercial bags that will keep fruit and vegetables for months without chilling: the bags release the ethylene as it forms. Look for them in supermarkets.

Potatoes keep best if they are cold (not frozen – frozen spuds rot), and dark and dry. When spuds get damp they rot too; when they're exposed to the light, they turn green – and poisonous – and start to sprout. One old-fashioned method of keeping spuds was to hill them in dry sand. I find a hessian sack hung up in a dark place works well enough to keep them through the winter until spring's new potatoes are ready for bandicooting.

Some useful preserves

Apples

Apples preserved in honey
Slice the fruit. Let the surface dry for a few hours, or wipe it with a cloth. Heat 1 kg of honey with 2 tablespoons of vinegar, bringing it slowly to the boil. Add a couple of cloves and a bit of cinnamon stick (both are optional). Add as much fruit as will fit. Simmer for twenty minutes. Take off the heat and seal into jars while it is hot.

Pickled crab apples
2 kg crab apples
7 cups white or cider vinegar
7 cups brown sugar or clear honey
1 tablespoon cloves
1 tablespoon cinnamon

Leave the stalks on the crab apples. Prick each one a few times with a fork. Boil the other ingredients for ten minutes. Add a few crab apples at a time, and boil till tender. Take them out, place them in a bottle and add more to the syrup until all are cooked. Boil the remaining syrup for five minutes and pour it over the fruit. Seal at once.

The apples should be left like this for at least three months. Eat them instead of olives or add them puréed to whipped cream for a crab-apple fool.

Red food-colouring improves the appearance of pickled crab apples; add a few drops if you like.

Apricots

Preserved apricots

Layer apricots and castor sugar in a pan. Don't add any water. Put it in the oven. Heat gently: the oven temperature should rise to no more than moderate. Leave the apricots there for 3 hours. Bottle while hot, and seal. There should be enough castor sugar and apricot juice to fill the jars to the top.

Beans

Beans can be dried: leave them on the bush till the pods are dry, then uproot the whole plant and bash it against a wall so the beans fall out on old newspaper on the ground. Gather the beans and keep them in a dry, dark place.

Stewed dried beans

Wash 500 g dried beans, but don't soak them. Sauté a sliced onion in half a cup of olive oil, add the beans and cook slowly until the beans have absorbed most of the oil. Add one litre of hot water, some garlic and a sprig of mint. Don't add salt: it will toughen the beans. Cover the pan, and stew as slowly as you can until all the liquid has been absorbed. Eat hot or cold with a drizzle of lemon juice.

Soybean curd

This can be made with other dried beans too – not just with soybeans. Dry soybeans in the oven until they are crisp. Grind them to flour in a flour mill or with a mortar and pestle. Add 8 cups of cold water to 2 cups of soyflour. Leave for half an hour, stirring a couple of times. Transfer to a pot, and bring to the boil – keep stirring, or it will stick on the bottom. Take off the heat and add 3 tablespoons of lemon juice, at once. Keep stirring. Let it cool down, but don't chill it in the fridge. Line a colander or sieve with cheesecloth or even a tea-towel. Tip the mixture in, and leave it overnight.

When it has set, store the bean curd in the fridge, covered with water.

Beetroot

Dried beetroot

Add this to boiled puddings and fruit cakes to make them lighter, moister and sweeter.

Grate the peeled beetroot. Dry in the sun or in a cool oven until it is perfectly dry. Store it in layers between greaseproof paper in a sealed jar.

Berries

The following method allows you to keep berries for stewing or jams without cooking them.

Take very clean, perfectly dry, unblemished berries. Place a layer of castor sugar in a jar, then a few berries, some more sugar, etc. Repeat this until the jar is full. The berries should be separated by the sugar and not touch each other. Seal well, making sure the sugar reaches right up to the top of the lid. Light will make the berries fade, and heat will make them ferment, so keep them in a dark, cool place.

The sugar will gradually extract the berry juice – as long as the jar stays sealed, there's no need to worry if it slowly turns liquid.

Use the berries in stews or jams, or serve them in their juice as a sauce over meringues, with cream.

Cabbage

Sauerkraut

This can be made with lettuce or young green beans.

Shred clean, crisp cabbage as finely as you can. Weigh out 2 kg in a bowl and sprinkle with 3 tablespoons of salt. Mix and leave until the cabbage wilts a bit – it is easier to press into a jar when it's soft and the juice has started to flow. Now press down as hard as you can in a pottery or opaque plastic jar. Try to force all air out; this will also force the juice out. Cover with a plastic bag half-filled with water – this should edge snugly round the cabbage so no air can get in at all. If there isn't enough juice within 24 hours to cover the cabbage, add salt and water: 1 cup of salt to 10 cups of water. Leave in a cool place for about six weeks. Then bring it to the boil in a saucepan with the juice, pack it into clean jars, and seal.

How to cook sauerkraut

Melt a knob of butter in a large pan and sauté a sliced onion till transparent. Rinse and drain the sauerkraut and cook it for 5 minutes. Add a grated apple, and simmer for 30 minutes. Moisten with a little stock or water. Bake in a moderate oven until tender.

Sauerkraut can be sprinkled with brown sugar or caraway seeds.

Dried cabbage

This is usually made from Chinese cabbage, though other cabbages can be used as well: select the tender inner leaves for drying. You can brush the leaves with lemon juice first – it keeps the cabbage's colour and softness better – but that isn't necessary. Leave the leaves in the sun for a couple of days until they are almost transparent. Take them in at night.

Brush the dried leaves with water and fill them with vinegar rice with a layer of pickles in the middle. Wrap this into a neat package and slice it thinly, so you see a green, then a white, and then a pickle layer.

Vinegar rice: for every two cups of rice add 2 tablespoons of white vinegar and half a tablespoon of sugar.

Capsicum

Paprika

Paprika or red pepper is dried ground capsicum. The hotter the variety, the hotter the pepper. Dry thin strips of capsicum in the sun or in a cool oven until they snap rather than bend. Grind them, using a blender, a mortar, or a grinder. The paprika may need to be dried again after grinding, then stored in a sealed jar in a dry, dark place.

Bottled capsicums

Choose ripe, red capsicums. Halve them, take out the seeds, lay them under the griller, cut side down, until the skins blister. You can then take the skins off. This step is essential and gives the capsicum a richer flavour. Make sure every scrap of skin has gone. This isn't as difficult as it sounds: the skin comes off quite easily. That is to say, it doesn't come off thin, green, shop-bought capsicums easily at all – so, if the capsicums aren't fat and ripe, don't try this recipe.

Now chop the peeled capsicum into very thin strips. Press these into small jars and add a few leaves of basil or tarragon, or even thyme if you don't have basil. Pour over enough olive oil to fill the jars – they shouldn't need much if you have squashed down the capsicum. Place the jars in a saucepan, and fil it up to their shoulders with well-salted water. Bring to the boil slowly, and boil for 20 minutes. Take off the heat, make sure the lids are tight, and keep in a cool cupboard.

These peppers can be used for cooking but they are also good simply as a salad, with a little lemon juice squeezed over them at the last minute, with salt if you like it, or with a few olives. They make a wonderful topping for very fresh home-made pasta – just the capsicum and oil and nothing else.

Celery

Celery salt

Celery is naturally salty and can be used to season dishes. Slice celery thinly and dry it in a cool oven or outdoors on aluminium foil – taking it indoors when it's dark or damp – or, of course, in a home dryer. Blend it or pound it in a mortar when it's dry enough to snap. Dry the powder again in a cool oven or in the midday sun for a couple of hours before storing it in sealed jars. Use it by the spoonful when needed to season soups, stews, breads, potato chips, etc.

Cherries

Spiced cherries, to eat like olives
1 kg cherries
1 kg sugar
half a litre of vinegar
3 cloves

Place the cherries in jars. Boil the rest of the ingredients together for 20 minutes. Pour it over the cherries and seal the jars at once. Leave them for 6 weeks before you eat them. These keep for at least a year.

This recipe is good with either blood-red cherries, yellow cherries, or sour Morello cherries – but the taste differs of course depending on the cherries used. I find the small Morello cherries the best.

Chillies

Chillies are best strung on cotton and hung around your kitchen: they look bright and last for a decade. One chilli crop is usually enough to last you for at least that long – unless you're passionate about burnt tongues.

Chillies in sherry

Cover fresh chillies with sherry. Use the chillies as needed, and the sherry in cooking.

Choko

Choko, to taste like pears

Simmer 3 peeled, cored and quartered chokos until tender in a syrup of 3 cups of sugar to 1 cup of water, flavoured with the juice of a lemon and a vanilla bean (taken out as soon as the fruit is cooked). Bottle the choko in the syrup and seal. Leave it for a month before eating.

Although these don't *really* taste like pears, this recipe does disguise the choko. This preserve is best used mixed with other fruit in tarts or hot fruit salads.

Corn

Dry the cobs; give them to the hens (a free-ranging hen needs about one cob a day) or boil them later in soups and stews. Dry the kernels – grind for cornflour. 'Milk' the kernels and freeze the juice – add to any soup or stew for protein and thickening. To store the corn on the stalk bend the top over so the rain runs away from the cob.

Parched corn

Leave some cobs on the stalk till they are dry, cut off with a knife then leave in a sealed container in the fridge – they should keep for three months or more. Fry them in oil like pop corn – they won't pop properly – they'll be more chewy but I prefer them like that. A bit of garlic added to the oil is good and a touch of pepper afterwards.

Hominy

Boil your corn or maize kernels until they are slushy: corn needs less cooking than maize, and young maize less than old. Add 1 teaspoon of salt to every 3 cups of slush, which should not be too moist: no liquid should run out when tilting the pan. Place it in sealed jars, and keep it in the fridge or a cool cupboard.

This keeps for months. When you want to serve it, heat it up and add butter to taste, with perhaps some cream and sugar. It can also be patted into thin cakes, and fried.

Corn vinegar
Take ripe corn and soak it overnight in twenty times its volume of water. Heat it gently until it starts to swell. Don't let it burst. Strain off the cooled liquid, and add 4 cups of sugar or honey to every kilogram of corn. Leave the liquid in a bottle without a lid in the sun, say on the window sill. It should turn into vinegar in about one month. Heat to boiling, take off the heat, bottle and seal.

Dandelions

Dandelion wine
Boil 2 litres of dandelion flowers for one hour in 4 litres of water with 1.25 kg sugar and the rinds of 2 oranges and 2 lemons. Cool till tepid, add the juice of the oranges and lemons, 50 g of raisins and 2 tablespoons of fresh yeast or its dried equivalent.

Leave for 24 hours, strain and bottle without screwing down the tops. Do this only when fermentation has finished, which may take a month or more.

Eggs

Chinese eggs
Take hard-boiled eggs, shell them and boil them again in equal parts sherry and soy sauce with a touch of honey and a little five-spice powder or aniseed. Bottle and seal.

These are beautiful sliced: brown, white and yellow. Keep in the fridge until needed.

Grapes

Verjuice
Green grape juice used to be called 'verjuice', and was once used extensively in cooking where we now tend to use lemon juice or tomatoes. Bottled grape juice is not the same. Press out green grapes and freeze the juice until it's needed. Make a sauce of half juice and half cream, boiled for five minutes with chopped parsley or coriander, to serve with veal or potatoes.

Grape jellies
These are delicate and incredibly good.

Take several bunches of grapes and boil them with a very little water until the grapes begin to burst. Take off the flame, press the grapes through a sieve, and reduce the pulp by half through rapid boiling.

Weigh what's left and add the same weight of sugar, and 250 g of apple pulp for every kilogram of grape juice. Cook this mixture until it begins to thicken and you can see the bottom of the pan as you stir. Pour it into a greased mould, and take it out when set. Dust with icing sugar, and store it wrapped in greaseproof paper in a sealed carton. These jellies can be sliced, or eaten whole with cream.

Lemons

Juiced lemons
Fill bottles with lemon juice and pour a little salad oil on top before sealing. Like this, the juice will keep for several months in the fridge.

Mandarins

Dried mandarins
Pierce each mandarin all over. Choose the small ones, which are sweet and seedy – not the giant Ellendales, which are soft and slushy. Leave them in the sun until they start to shrivel – this usually takes about three days, more or less depending on the weather. Prepare a syrup by boiling 1 cup of sugar in one-third of a cup of water with a dessertspoon red wine vinegar, a grate of fresh ginger and a couple of cloves. After 10 minutes, add the mandarins. Take it off the heat, leave it overnight, then boil the lot again. Bottle and seal. Leave for three months before using.

Mangos

Superior sauce
4 mangos, peeled and sliced
sugar to taste
brandy
Combine the ingredients. Bottle and seal. Keep for at least one month. This can be used as a sauce with cold meat, hot pork or icecream. It can also be added to an equal amount of champagne and drunk – with joy.

Milk

Simple fresh cheese
This isn't cottage cheese, and it isn't cream cheese – it's simply fresh cheese.

Fill a bowl with milk; leave for two days at room temperature. (This assumes your room is comfortable – if it's stinking hot, keep it in a cool cupboard instead.) The milk should thicken slightly without going bad. You can hasten this by adding a junket tablet, but if you have enough patience there's no need for that. Pour this into a cloth – I use a clean tea-towel, doubled over – and hang it in a cool place, like over the bath, until the liquid has run out and the cheese is firm. Serve with fresh fruit, fresh fruit puree, cream or sugar.

Fresh cheeses can be kept to mature: rub them in wax and leave them for six months. Or keep them in brine made with 3 cups of water and 3 cups of salt. They don't have the same texture as a 'proper' matured cheese – but they're still very good. I like them best after about three weeks: firm, but slightly soapy; sliceable, but still with a fine, fresh flavour.

Mulberry

Wine

Mash your berries, and strain. For every cup of juice, add 1 cup of sugar and 1 cup of water. Mix, put in bottles, and leave the tops off. The wine should start to ferment within a few days. Seal when the fermentation has stopped. Keep for at least one year or it will be too sweet.

Oranges

Green-orange preserve

This is a very good way of using fruit that drops off in wet weather. Other citrus can also be used, especially limes, mandarins, and kumquats.

Take whole green oranges, just before they start to show colour. Stick a knife down the centre and cut out the middle – just like coring an apple. This should get rid of the seeds. Soak the fruit in salty water for 24 hours, using about 3 cups of water to half a cup of salt. Drain, and wash well in fresh water. Boil the fruit in a large pan of water, adding 1 teaspoon of bicarbonate of soda to every 6 cups of water. When a skewer will easily prick the skins, take them out and wash them in cold water inside and out. Don't cook the fruit for so long that they turn squashy, or they will become too hard in the syrup.

Boil 2 kg of sugar for 10 minutes in 1 litre of water to which the juice of 2 lemons has been added. Pour over the fruit, leave it for 24 hours. Re-boil the syrup until a little sets in cold water, add the fruit and bring to the boil again. Bottle while hot, and seal.

Peaches

Peach leather

Skin and stone your peaches, either yellow or white-fleshed ones. Sieve, and spread them over a greased tray. Dry this in a cool oven or in the sun (taking it inside overnight) until it is hard. Peel this away from the pan, wrap it in greaseproof paper, and store it in airtight jars till needed. This can be eaten as it is – an excellent sweet for children – or reconstituted by soaking it in boiling water until it turns soft again.

Other fruits – like apples, apricots, pears, etc. – all make good fruit leathers.

Pears

Pears dry easily: peel, quarter and core them, brush them with lemon juice, and leave them in the sun till chewy.

Peas

Dry them for soup or stews: just leave them in the sun until they're hard, or let them dry in the pod on the vine. Grind the dried peas in a flour mill or coffee grinder for pea flour. Add it to stews, etc. for thickening, or to bread for flavour and protein.

Pea flour chappattis
Add some water to pea flour to make a batter. Roll this out very thinly, and fry in very hot oil. Eat hot.

Plums

Dried plums are prunes – usually special varieties of 'prune' plums that dry well. Other plums can be easily dried too: remove the stone, spread the halves in the sun, and wait, keeping them away from the rain and the dew.

Chinese salted plums
These are supposed to prevent travel sickness. I find they make me more nauseous, not less; but they may work for other people.

Take small plums. Leave the seeds in. Prick them several times and leave them in the sun for three days, taking care that no dew or rain falls on them. Now pack them in salt, so that no plum touches another. Leave for three weeks, take them out and wash. Leave them in the sun for another day or two, until they're quite dry. Pack them in a sealed jar.

Plum sauce
3 kg plums, preferably dark red
2 kg raw sugar
1 teaspoon whole black peppers
4 cups vinegar
10 cloves garlic
1 teaspoon salt
1 teaspoon ground ginger
1 chopped onion
Boil all the ingredients until the stones separate from the plums. Bottle and seal. This keeps for years.

Potatoes

Potato cheese
Take 2 kg mashed potatoes, very finely mashed. Add half a litre of sour milk or cream, and beat well. Leave this in a china dish covered with a tea-towel in a cool place (not the fridge) for four days. Knead the mixture well, then place small rounds of it in muslin or other plain cloth to drain for two days. Rub the cheeses over with butter. They should mature for at least three weeks – and will keep for years.

Pumpkin

Substitue mashed pumpkin for one-third of the flour in bread and cakes: it makes them light and moist. Do the same with pikelets, then sprinkle them with sugar or spread them with honey – wonderful. Mashed pumpkin can be frozen. Use pumpkin chunks instead of potato pieces in potato or fish cakes. Try baked pumpkin with a sauce made of cream and French mustard boiled for three minutes.

Pumpkin flour
Pumpkin flour is good added to cakes: 1 cup of pumpkin flour to 4 cups ordinary flour. Cut the pumpkin in thin slices and dry it in a slow oven until crisp – avoid browning. Crush with a rolling pin or in a blender until it's powdery.

Mock ginger
This is an old colonial standby.
   Cut your pumpkin into neat slices, sprinkle them with salt, and leave them overnight. Pour off the juice. Add a syrup made of 2 cups of sugar to 1 cup of water with 1 dessertspoon of grated or powdered ginger. Boil this for an hour, pour it over the pumpkin and leave until cold. Pour off the syrup, and repeat at least six times. The pumpkin should look as though it is starting to candy, changing colour with the repeated applications of boiling syrup. Put the lot in the oven until the pumpkin is cooked. The outside will be crystallised and crunchy but the inside will be soft. Place it in clean jars when it's still hot, adding a shaving of lemon zest. Seal, and don't use for at least three months. This keeps for years.

Pumpkin chutney
This is very good. Don't let the blandness of mashed pumpkin put you off. The longer you leave it, the better it gets.
1 kg pumpkin
500 g tomatoes
500 g chopped onions
700 g brown sugar
2 teaspoons each of black peppercorns, whole allspice, and ground ginger
6 cloves chopped garlic
1 litre red wine vinegar
   Slice the pumpkin in thin neat pieces. Skin the tomatoes (Leave them in boiling water for a few seconds, and the skin will come off easily.) Add all the ingredients together and simmer – don't boil – until thick. Stir often, as this chutney sticks easily. Bottle while hot.

Rhubarb

Rhubarb 'champagne'
1 kg rhubarb
5 litres cold water
1 dessertspoon white wine vinegar
1 sliced lime or lemon
500 g sugar

Chop the rhubarb, and add the other ingredients. Leave this alone for 24 hours. Stir until the sugar dissolves. Strain, bottle. The 'champagne' is ready to drink in about five days. If you keep it any longer, open the bottles every day to release the pressure or they may explode.

Roses

Rosehip vinegar

Rosehips are high in vitamin C. But vitamin C is destroyed by cooking – so I use this recipe without cooking.

Take as many deep red rosehips as the garden or wild briars will supply. (It doesn't matter if they are withered.) Chop them roughly. Just cover them with cider vinegar. Sweeten with honey to taste. (Note that if the hips are sweet it may not need any sugar.) Leave for at least three weeks before using.

Take one teaspoon dissolved in hot water every day, preferably before breakfast.

Strawberries

Strawberry and passionfruit jelly

Take 3 cups of apple juice, undiluted. Add, for every cup of apple juice, 1 cup of passionfruit pulp, 2 cups of strawberries and 1 cup of sugar or very pale honey. Boil for an hour, or until a little sets in cold water. Bottle while hot, and seal.

This is a wonderfully coloured, very gentle jelly – perhaps the best topping for pikelets there is.

Sunflowers

Sunflower butter

Shell the seeds, place them on a tray in the oven and cook them at a moderate heat until they start to smell caramelly and are just beginning to change colour. Take them out and grind them in the blender – or even a coffee or flour mill – and there you are. Sunflower butter is a bit blander than peanut butter. It is best with honey, and it makes a good dip sauce with a bit of lemon juice and perhaps some salt added to it.

Actually, the whole sunflower head can be eaten, if you pick it young enough. They can be pickled while they are still soft, or eaten like artichokes.

Sunflower artichokes

Pick your sunflower heads when they can still be squeezed without feeling any seeds – the smaller the better. Steam them for twenty minutes. Toss them in a dressing of olive oil and lemon juice. Eat hot. They are also good with melted butter with garlic and lemon juice.

Tomatoes

Tomatoes are one of the few crops I can't feel 'seasonal' about. I want them all year round. That means preserving them.

Preserved uncooked tomatoes

Take ripe, firm, small tomatoes. They must have no bruise or blemish at all. Make sure they are clean and quite dry.

Place them in a tall, deep jar, one at a time – again, make sure they do not squash, bruise or split. Cover with oil right to the top of the jar. Seal. Keep in the fridge until needed. These will keep up to six months or even longer.

Tomato paste

There are dozens of ways of making tomato paste. Try chopping the tomatoes, and simmer them without added water until they are thick and bubble like magma: great bursts of bubbles that spread over the kitchen. Spread the mixture on aluminium foil and leave it in the sun until it is dry – taking it indoors in wet weather or overnight (to keep the dew off). Now roll the sticky mixture into balls, dip each ball in a cup of oil and store them in sealed glass jars in the fridge. Take them out as you need them. Otherwise, just stuff the paste in a jar and cover the lot with oil – though this can result in an uneven surface as you use it, some of which may not be covered in oil, causing you to lose some of the paste to fungus.

If you don't want to dry the paste in the sun, boil it down as far as possible, after adding one tablespoon of white vinegar or half a teaspoon of citric acid for every four cups of tomatoes. Pack the thick purée into glass jars, and cover it with a film of oil. Place the jars in a tray of water in the oven and cook until the water just boils. Leave till cool and seal.

At the simmering stage, the paste can be flavoured with garlic, black pepper, or very finely chopped basil or thyme.

Sun-dried tomatoes

These are wonderful.

Cut your tomatoes in half and leave them on trays in the sun for three days to a week until they're dry – they should be chewy rather than crisp. Pack them in jars with a little garlic, basil, or fresh thyme. Pack them down hard, then fill the jars with olive oil. Put the tops on the jars and keep until needed. Add the tomato and oil to soups and stews.

Vine leaves

Vine leaves in brine

These can be used for stuffed vine leaves during winter. Take 3 cups of salt. Add 1 dessertspoon of water. The salt should now dissolve – if it doesn't, add more water, drop by drop. As soon as there are no more salt crystals, pour the brine into a jar closely packed with layers of vine leaves. (The vine leaves should be soaked in fresh water for an hour before they are used.) Seal, and keep in a cool place till needed.

Zucchini

Zucchini leather
Cut the zucchini into thin strips, dip in boiling water, and dry in the sun until they are rubbery. Store them between greaseproof paper. Use them in stews or eat them by themselves. You can also use them instead of crackers for dips or with peanut sauce.

Chapter 9

The backyard supermarket

Most products become mysterious with packaging. Moisturiser, shampoo, or gourmet mustard: stick them in a fancy bottle with a professional label, and they seem impossible to produce at home. Actually, most are even better made at home: fresher, with a higher quality, and without preservatives and artificial colours.

But don't let this chapter tempt you too much. Whilst most of the necessities of life – and many of its luxuries – can be grown and made at home, total self-sufficiency is hard work. Bits of it, though, are fun.

After-shave spice

Take 1 handful of fragrant rose petals, 1 dessertspoonful of cloves, 3 crushed bayleaves and 1 cup of wine vinegar.

Bring to the boil, simmer for ten minutes, take off the heat and leave till cool. Strain and bottle in a well-sealed jar. Leave for at least two weeks before using.

Bath oil

Bath oils are rarely literally oils: a few drops of oil are merely added for perfume, as few oils disperse in water and a pure oil additive would leave a greasy mess on both the bath and its occupant.

To make a simple 'bath oil' take the petals of any fragrant flower – dianthus are excellent, as are musk roses, carnations, jasmine, pittosporum or boronia flowers – or any fragrant leaves, like scented geranium, mints or verbena. Chop them roughly, place in a jar and add a sliver of soap. Fill with water, put the lid on and leave in a hot place like the bathroom window sill until wanted.

Shake the bottle every time you pass. To use it, just pour some of the scented soapy water into the bath.

oils & vinegars

SSS

chutneys / preserves

homebrews

FIG JAM

wine (plum)

Home produce

Beer

Hops are an easily grown, prolific, deciduous vine, grown either from seed or a bit of root. We grow them over our dunny down the back.

Simple hop beer

Boil, for half an hour, 500 g hop flowers with a piece of raw ginger in 6 litres of water. Add 1 kg sugar, bring to the boil again, take off the heat, cover, and let stand overnight. Strain, bottle and . . . start drinking after a few days. Don't keep this beer for more than two weeks.

Ginger beer

Bring to the boil 4 cups of water, 2 sliced lemons, and 1 cup of sugar. Add a bit of ginger root or powdered ginger. When cool, add a pinch of dried yeast.

Leave for 24 hours. Strain and bottle. This is ready in 24 hours in hot weather, or a week in cool weather.

Cloves

Clove pinks or dianthus, or clove-scented carnations are a simple way to get a clove flavour. Simply cover the fresh flowers in castor sugar, and use the clove-scented sugar where needed. Don't worry if the sugar dissolves in the jar with the flowers – you'll just have clove syrup instead.

Cocoa

Carob 'cocoa' or 'coffee'

Cut ripe carob pods into small pieces, remove the seeds, and then toast the pieces of pod until they're quite dry. Either grind them in a blender or bash the pieces with a hammer in a paper bag. The resulting powder is then sieved: the fine powder can be used as carob flour in cakes and biscuits, or it can be used like coffee grounds. The coarser bits need to be brewed like tea: put them in a saucepan with either water or milk and heat slowly. Strain when the liquid is dark enough.

Coffee

While most Australian gardens can't reproduce commercial coffee growing conditions (wet and mountainous), any area that has no more than light frosts (or a sheltered spot against a white, north facing wall, say, in colder areas) can grow a couple of coffee bushes. Seed is available sporadically from several suppliers, and bushes can also be bought occasionally from specialist nurseries.

Growing coffee

The coffee bush can grow to an enormous size. They are usually kept pruned, though, to about two to three metres, and can even be smaller if space is limited. The bushes have shiny leaves, dark and leathery, with clusters of highly scented white flowers.

Coffee bushes need moist but well drained soil, with plenty of organic matter, and a good nitrogen/phosphorous balance to keep the bush producing heavily. A spot with broken light, say under taller trees, is excellent to start off your coffee bushes: they will be protected from both frost and strong light.

Although the bushes may survive heavy frost, the flowers may be burnt off. Try sheltering them with hessian sacking overnight, or keep them watered with micro-jets on clear starry nights when you can smell a frost.

Producing coffee

Each coffee flower produces a two-lobed fruit, the coffee berry. This is green at first, then red, then bright scarlet. At that stage they should be picked.

Each lobe of the fruit contains a seed: the coffee bean. These need to be separated from the berry, which is usually done by a process of fermentation. But for home use it is enough to soak the berry in water until the outside can be removed easily. This should take three to four days.

Dry the beans thoroughly in the sun for a week or two till the beans turn bluey green. Now spread the beans on trays and turn them once or twice a day, bringing them inside if necessary, away from rain and dew. When they are dried, rub them vigorously together to take off the outer skins.

The beans are then roasted at about 200°C till they have caramelised slightly, turning yellow then brown. Don't overcook them. You will know when your coffee is roasted sufficiently by the smell as well as the colour: take your coffee from the oven when the fragrance fills the kitchen.

The beans should now be brittle and incredibly fragrant. By this time they will have lost about one-fifth of their weight. Grind them in a coffee grinder or in a blender, preferably just before you are going to use them. If you prefer to grind a lot at once, keep it in a sealed jar or, better still, keep it sealed and frozen until needed. Whole beans should also be kept in a sealed jar in a cool, dry place.

You will vary the flavour of your coffee by the amount of time you take to dry it, roast it, and ferment it. The flavour also changes with the type of beans and with the growing conditions.

Finely ground coffee can be used by simply placing a dessertspoon in a saucepan, pouring over two cups of boiling water, leaving it for a minute, then straining the liquid back into the cups leaving the grounds behind. Coarser coffee needs to be heated to just below boiling point – or use one of the many coffee-making apparatuses on the market.

Coffee substitutes

The best artificial 'coffees' come from plants rich in natural sugars, which roast and 'caramelise' well. It's worth experimenting. Coffee's popularity is partly due to its flavour remaining long after it's been roasted and ground. Substitutes lose their flavour faster, but home-made such drinks are fresh.

With all coffee substitutes, try to use organic ingredients: some pesticides and herbicide elements can be even more harmful after heating. Try mixing different grounds together: beetroot with sunflower is good; acorn goes well with a little sweet potato or chicory; or add barley to any of the roasts if you want a 'coffee' that isn't so strongly flavoured.

Don't go overboard with the roasting – ingredients should be brown and crisp, but not blackened. A black roast will give you a bitter cup.

Whether grain or root, the best roast is done as slowly as possible. If you don't want to use your oven for such a long time just to roast 'coffee', you can partially dry your ingredients, place them in a sealed container, then put them back in whenever you use the oven again.

Acorn coffee

Frequently used in Europe during World War II, this has a bad reputation as a tasteless 'coffee'. But it is tasteless only when it's stale – fresh acorn 'coffee' is very good.

Most acorns need long boiling or soaking to remove their bitterness. Taste them first. If they are bitter, cover with boiling water and keep changing the water every morning until it tastes sweet.

Then dry the acorns in the oven till they are turning brown and begin to caramelise. You can tell when this is happening: the kitchen should be filled with the sweet scent of roasting. Take out the acorns (they should be dry and crisp) and grind them in a blender – or put them in a paper bag and bash with a hammer. If you need to store them, freeze them at this stage or keep them in a sealed container. However, the longer roast acorns are kept, the blander they'll taste.

To make acorn 'coffee' pour a cup of boiling water over the coarse grounds, leave for two minutes, then strain or pour off the liquid leaving the sodden grounds behind. Re-heat if necessary, but don't boil.

Beetroot 'coffee'

This must be used fresh, or it is tasteless. Peel beetroots, cut into halves or quarters, and dry in a cool oven till crisp. This may take 12 hours or more. Grind in a pepper mill, mouli or blender. If they won't grind, the pieces aren't crisp enough. Place the grounds in a saucepan, about a dessertspoon per person, and pour boiling water on it. Leave for 2 minutes. Strain or pour off carefully. The resulting drink will be sweet and thick, like Turkish coffee, and brown rather than red. It is a wonderful winter after-dinner drink.

Chicory 'coffee'

Chicory has always been a popular coffee alternative: like coffee it keeps its flavour for a long time. You can also add a little chicory to any of the other 'coffees'. Chicory is a lovely perennial in the garden: it comes up every year, with tall blue stalks of flowers over most of summer. Every year there are more roots – and a few seedlings as well. The root can be dug at any time, but it is sweetest in autumn.

Chicory 'coffee' is made the same way as the other coffee substitutes: roast slices of the scrubbed root, then grind, and pour boiling water on it. Use one dessertspoonful of the grounds for every cup of water. Chicory 'coffee' can also be made with milk: use cold milk and gradually heat it with the chicory; strain, and serve.

Kurrajong 'coffee'

Kurrajong 'coffee' is also good – though like beetroot coffee it must be drunk fresh. Dig up a thick root and scrape it clean – you needn't peel it. Chop it and treat as for beetroot. Kurrajong roots store a lot of sugar, and like chicory and beetroot they caramelise well.

Sunflower 'coffee'

This is made by roasting sunflower seeds in a slow oven until they are brittle – there's no need to hull them – then grinding them finely. Use two dessertspoons of ground sunflower seeds per cup of boiling water. Let the grains settle, and strain. You may need to re-heat it. Sunflower coffee has a fine, rich flavour when freshly roasted and ground, but it becomes insipid after a day or two.

Wattle 'coffee'

Many wattle seeds are bitter. Taste them. If they are sweet, dry them, grind them, and use them like other 'coffees'.

Curry powder

A mild curry powder can be made from the leaves of the curry plant, *Helichrysum augustifolium*. This shrubby perennial bush grows to about half a metre, with intensely scented silver leaves. Don't expect a rich curry from curry plant leaves alone – other spices will still be needed. But for an elusive curry taste to mayonnaise, sauces, etc. curry plant is wonderful. Curry plant tolerates light frost once it is established.

Deodorant

Neither of these recipes will stop perspiration like commercial deodorants claim to do. They will, however, help prevent an unpleasant body odour.

Recipe 1

Take 2 cups of cider vinegar, bring to the boil, and add 2 cups of as many of the following mixed ingredients as you can get: sage leaves, witch-hazel leaves (*Hamamelis virginiana*), rosemary leaves, and parsley leaves. Take off the heat. Bottle and leave for 2 weeks before using. Dab wherever it's needed.

Recipe 2

Melt 2 tablespoons of beeswax with 2 tablespoons of olive oil, half a teaspoon of lavender oil, and half a teaspoon of rosemary oil. Pour into an old deodorant container and rub onto your skin when cool. (*Note*: this deoderant will also help keep away mosquitoes.)

Room deodorant

Steep, for two days in a sealed container, 1 cup of chopped lemon rind – fresh if possible – in 2 cups of tea. Shake once a day. Strain and spray. Alternatively, steep 1 cup of chopped mint in 2 cups of tea, shaking once a day.

Spray these with an old-fashioned pump sprayer, still readily available for a couple of dollars.

Dye

Most dyes require a mordant to 'fix' the colour: to make it deeper or richer, or more permanent. Mordants include salts of alum – available at chemists – chrome, tin, and copper.

Dyeing wool or cotton fibres

There are many complicated procedures for home dyeing. The following procedure is extremely simplified – but it works.

Take the materials you want to use for dyeing and soak them in cold water, overnight or longer. Bark should be soaked for about one month. Use soft water – tank water if you have it. Use only enough water to cover the dyeing material: you want a very strong solution for dyeing.

Now boil the materials: at least 45 minutes for petals, and one to two hours for leaves – depending on how tough they are. Leave for 24 hours and boil again. Strain thoroughly.

Now soak your wool or cotton (synthetics won't dye) in the dyeing solution. Work to a general rule of 1 litre of dyeing solution to every 25 g of cloth. Bring it all to simmering point. Take out the wool and add your mordant – say 1 level teaspoon for every 100 g of wool. Mix well. Replace the wool. Simmer for 1 to 24 hours: the longer the time, the more intense the colour. Never boil though, as boiling may destroy the colour.

Now either let the wool cool in the dyeing solution or take it out and rinse it in hot, then warm, then cold water.

If you enjoy dyeing there is no reason not to experiment with every plant in your garden, using changes of mordants and scraps of wool or other materials for testing.

Dyes without mordants

A few dyes will colour cloth without needing a mordant: for example henna red or walnut skins, which give a deep rich brown.

Scrub bloodwood

The sap of the scrub bloodwood, *Baloghia lucida*, can be used as an indelible red dye. Scrub bloodwood is a Queensland and New South Wales rainforest tree, with dark green leathery leaves. To extract the sap, make a thin, shallow cut in the bark. The sap should flow slowly for the next 12 to 24 hours.

Eucalypti

Many eucalyptus species give indelible dyes when the leaves are boiled without a mordant, though the resulting colours are usually soft rather than bright. Lemon-scented gum leaves (*E citriodotra*) will produce a mild fawn-coloured dye without a mordant when boiled with wool or cotton, though the addition of alum will give a better result. Pinks can be obtained by boiling red or green kangaroo-paw leaves, blue peppermint gum leaves (*E cinerea*), or the flowers and leaves of Sturt's desert pea.

Indigo is produced from the indigo plant, *Indigofera tinctoria*, which grows wild in Queensland and the Northern Territory.

Indigofera australis is a common ornamental native shrub, with glowing sprays of bright purple flowers. The leaves give a very pale rather dingy dye, though the quality appears to vary from plant to plant.

Method   Leave freshly picked leaves in warm water to ferment for 24 hours, simmer for half an hour, then add a little slaked lime and dip the cloth in the liquid. This may have to be repeated several times to get a deep colour, depending on the strength of the indigo.

Lichens

Dyes from most lichens don't need mordants either, though they give a richer colour if one is used. The cloth should be simmered with the lichen for several hours. Colours range from yellow through browns and reds.

Brighter colours have traditionally been made from lichens by soaking them in urine or half-strength household ammonia for about one month, then soaking the cloth in the resulting liquid. This method gives deeper reds and browns as well as blues. Some wood-rotting fungi can be used in the same way, giving various colours.

Woad

Woad is one of the most famous dyes, used by the ancient Britons to colour their skin. Woad (*Isatis tinctoria*) is a small, pretty herb with masses of tiny yellow flowers in mid-summer. To make dye from it, strip off the leaves, pound them well, and store them in plastic bags until they start to ferment. Then simmer them in a solution of quicklime and water. The quantities depend on the growing conditions of the plant: you will need to experiment.

Other plants

Other plant dyes which don't need mordants include dandelion, which gives a pale pink colour; ladies bedstraw, which gives a pale rusty red; elder leaves and stalks, which give a greyish blue colour; and coreopsis flowers, which give a clear yellow colour if boiled with bleached wool or linen.

Dyes with mordants

The colours given here are only approximate. Both cultivars and growing conditions can vary, and so will the colour produced by any particular plant and mordant.

Eucalypts
- Apple box (*E bridgesiana*) with alum: red
- Bastard Tallowood (*E planchiniana*) with copper and iron: black
- Blue peppermint (*E cinerea*) with alum: red
- Flooded gum (*E grandis*) with iron: black
- Mahogany gum (*E botryiodes*) with alum: fawn
- Mountain gum (*E dalrympleana*) with alum: red
- Narrow leafed ironbark (*E creba*) with alum: fawn
- Red box (*E polyanthemos*) with alum: red
- Red flowering gum (*E ficifolia*) with iron: black
- Red ironbark (*E sideroxylon*) with alum: orange
- River red gum (*E camaldulensis*) with alum: orange
- Silver peppermint (*E risdonni*) with iron and copper: black
- Sugar gum (*E cladpocalyx*) with alum: yellow
- Victorian blue gum (*E bicostata*) with alum: orange
- Brown stringybark (*E baxteri*) with copper: brown

Wattles
- Black wattle (*Acacia mearnsi*) alum: light brown
- Cunningham's wattle (*A cunninghamii*) with tin: gold colour
- Golden wattle (*A prominens*) with alum: gold colour

Other native dye plants
- Banksia (*Banksia integrifolia*) with alum: gold
- Bauhina (*Bauhinia carroni*) with chrome: brownish yellow
- Native cherry leaves and stems (*Exocarpus cupressiformis*) with alum: light brown
- River she-oak (*Casuarina cuninghamiana*) with copper: green

Exotic dye plants
- Dandelion (*Taraxacum officinale*) with alum: reddish purple
- Elder (*Sambuccus nigre*) with alum and salt: lavender to pale purple
- Horsetail (*Esquisetum*) with alum: grey
- Onion skin with chrome: black to dark brown
- Rhododendron with chrome: various shades of brown
- Tansy with chrome and cream of tartar: orange

Face wash

Oily skin
Take a handful of yarrow, steep it in a glass of boiling water until cool, and add the juice of two lemons.

Dry-skin moisturiser
Mix 20 g of ground almonds with half a litre of rose water – rain water may be used instead. Leave for half an hour, filter through fine muslin, and add half a teaspoon of sugar and tincture of benzoin (obtainable from a chemist). Bottle and seal until needed.

Normal skin
Cover a handful of chamomile flowers and half a cup of pulped strawberries with a cup of boiling water. Cool, strain and use.

To prevent wrinkles
Cover a cup of poppy petals with half a cup of boiling water. Let them cool, then strain and bottle till needed. I have tried this recipe but can't vouch for its effectiveness. It does make a pleasant wash for the skin though.

Ginger

Ginger can be grown in any frost-free spot that's fertile, moist and well-drained. Plant a bit of root and wait. It may take a season or two for the new roots to be big enough to harvest.

In colder areas, try ginger mint: rampant and with a wonderful flavour, it's even better in your ginger beer and stir-fry vegetables than ginger root; or you could even try ginger-scented geranium.

Hair conditioner

Take a handful of rosemary or chamomile. Pour over a cup of boiling vinegar. Let it steep for half an hour, add two cups of water, then use it as a final rinse for your hair.

Hand cream

Recipe 1
Take clear lard. (Fat melted slowly in twice as much water and strained to remove impurities. Good lard doesn't smell of animal fat.) Melt it and pour a very thin layer into a glass jar. Quickly add either jasmine or fragrant rose buds. Wait till the lard has set then repeat the procedure till the jar is full. Leave for a couple of days then melt the lard again and strain it.

Repeat with more flowers, and continue the procedure until the lard is strongly perfumed.

Rub on your hands after washing or gardening.

Recipe 2

Take a cupful of any fragrant flower: boronia, jasmine, rose petals, orange blossom. Place them in a saucepan with 500 Ml bland oil, and steep gently for half an hour. *Do not bring to the boil.* Take off the heat and add 50 g of melted beeswax. Mix well. Store in a sealed jar.

Mustard

Mustard can be grown from mustard seed sold in supermarkets. The seed will be ready to harvest in about three months or less, depending on the climate.

English mustard

Take ground mustard seeds, add a touch of white pepper, ground ginger, and chilli powder if you want a hot mustard, then make up a quarter of the bulk with fine rice flour. Add enough ground tumeric to colour it bright yellow. Moisten with white wine vinegar.

French mustard

Steep the mustard seed in vinegar overnight before you dry it and grind it. Now add as much red wine vinegar as needed to make a paste, along with a little honey, ground black pepper and cinnamon to flavour.

Nutmeg

While nutmeg is strictly a tropical crop, the dried powdered leaves of the native *Backhousia myrtifolia*, otherwise known as the never-break tree, can be used as a substitute. These grow wild in fringe rainforest gullies in N.S.W. They need good soil and moisture and protection from heavy frost. During droughts they become defoliated. However, they grow back as soon as it rains. They are a medium-sized, small-leafed tree with tiny white flowers and would look lovely in a sheltered corner or a garden. They respond well to pruning.

Pepper

Black, white and green peppers are obtained form the same vine, *Piper nigrum*. Green pepper is just that. Black peppers are picked green and left to ferment in heaps for a few days, then spread on mats in the sun for about twenty hours until they shrivel and turn brown or black.

White pepper is produced from ripe berries, picked when they are just about to turn red. They are packed in sacks and soaked in slow-flowing water for about a week, then trampled to rub off the outer hull. They are then dried till they turn creamy white, and ground.

In sheltered spots pepper grows as far south as Sydney. For colder climates the best way to grow pepper is as a pot plant. Alternatively, find a thick canopy tree – avocados are excellent, or even bay trees – and grow the pepper vine up the tree, under its sheltering branches.

Left to itself pepper grows to about 10 metres, with a stem diameter as thick as your thumb. Hard pruning will not only keep it in check, but promote lateral branching – and more pepper.

Commercial pepper vines are mostly propagated from cuttings. Cuttings bear after one to three years, reaching full production in about eight years. Vines grown from seed may take six or seven years to bear. You should eventually get up to 2 kg of pepper from each vine.

As soon as your vine is as tall as your finger, start to hill it up, so that the vine is almost covered, preferably with good compost. This will encourage more shoots – and more pepper. Feed the vine well with a high-nitrogen phosphorous mix – a twice yearly application of hen manure is excellent – to encourage leaf production. Make sure the soil around it is kept moist but not waterlogged.

There are at least two native species of pepper. *P novae hollandiae* is native to subtropical Queensland and Northern New South Wales rainforests; *P rothianum* is native to Queensland tropical rainforests. They are both climbers, and the fruit can be used in the same way as that of the introduced species.

The pepper tree (*Schnius molle*) does not produce genuine pepper, although the seeds look pepper-shaped and the leaves smell peppery when rubbed. They can be dried for a mild pepper flavour. The pepper tree will only tolerate very light frost, but is extremely drought hardy and fast growing. It grows very easily from seed.

Home-made red pepper can be made by drying any of the capsicums: the hotness of the condiment will depend on whether you are using capsicum or one of the chillies. Cut the chilli or capsicum in half, leave the seeds in, and dry in the sun or a cool oven. When they are quite dry and brittle pulverise them in a blender or pound them with a mortar and pestle, then seal in an airtight jar till needed.

The mountain pepper bush (*Tasmania lanceolata*) is native to Tasmania, Victoria and New South Wales. It can be very attractive, with long leaves and bright red young branches. Both the leaves and the fruit can be dried and ground as an alternative to 'red pepper'. The fruit in particular is extremely hot.

The related native pepper tree (*Tasmania insipida*) is a rainforest shrub, less hardy than mountain pepper, and native to Queensland and New

South Wales. The fruit should be soaked in water and the flesh removed, the seed dried and ground for a very hot 'red pepper'.

Perfume

Any fragrant flowers can be very simply made into home-made perfumes either by steeping them in oil or alcohol or by following the attar of roses recipe given below. The oil-based recipes can be used as bath oils too, or as a fragrant after-shower rub.

Pick the flowers for perfume-making in the early morning if you can, when the dew is still on them. Choose flowers that are just opening rather than fully blown ones. If your are adding herbs, they are usually most fragrant just before the flowers open.

Start off with the classic perfume flowers – rose, gardenia, magnolia, and apple blossom – then experiment with your own garden favourites like leon blossom, dianthus, sweet pea, or clematis, perhaps.

And, of course, the natives can be added to any fragrant garden flowers you have: orange blossom, lilac, scented geranium leaves, bay leaves, Chilean jasmine flowers, a few conifer leaves, daphne, gardenia, lilac, lemon verbena, magnolia, or mock orange – if it is scented you can use it.

Add a touch of richeness with some herbs or spices to deepen the fragrance of your mixture: nutmeg, bay leaves, mace, cardamom, and lemon grass, for example.

Attar of roses

Attar of roses was traditionally made with damask roses, but any fragrant flower, rose or otherwise, will give you a concentrated perfume. I use highly scented hybrid musk roses as well as dianthus flowers and jasmine buds.

Choose your petals or flowers in the morning, after the dew has evaporated and they are at their most fragrant. Make sure the petals are unblemished and the flowers just before their prime.

Now take a pottery jar or casserole, unglazed if you can find one – not glass and not metal. A clean terracotta pot works well, with a well fitting plate weighted down as a lid.

Line your pot with petals, sprinkle with a thin layer of coarse salt or rock salt. Alternate these layers till the pot is full. Put the lid on the pot. If it doesn't fit tightly, seal it with plasticine, 'blu-tack' or candle wax. Leave it undisturbed in a cool, dark cupboard for at least three weeks, then strain it through a fine cloth. Pour with fluid into a glass bottle and put the lid on. Stand in the sun for six weeks to settle.

At the end of this time you will have the concentrated perfume of whatever flower you chose. Two drops will perfume a litre of water. Use it in cooking, when washing, or keep it for yourself.

Oil-based perfume

Take fragrant leaves or petals, put them in a glass jar and cover with a bland oil – like olive oil. Add a little brandy. Seal, and place in a warm spot like a window sill for at least three weeks, shaking every day. Use as required.

Alcohol-based perfume

As above, but cover the leaves or petals with brandy alone.

Saffron

This is a cooler climate spice. Saffron comes from the dried stigmas of the flowers of the bulb *Crocus sativus*. True saffron is exquisite, deeply perfumed, and hardly resembles the artificial saffron mostly sold today. Probably the only reason saffron isn't commercially grown in Australia is the expense of harvesting. Each flower bears three stigma, and each stigma must be picked individually by hand.

Crocus sativus is a small, decorative bulbous perennial, about 30 to 50 cm high, with violet to blue lilly-shaped flowers and vivid orange-red stigmas. It is autumn flowering, and won't tolerate frost while blooming, though the plants themselves are reasonably frost tolerant. They like light, well drained soil with a low rainfall – about 400 mm a year.

Saffron is propagated from the young cornlets produced each year at the base of the bulb. It can also be grown from seed, though seedlings may take three to four years to flower.

As soon as the crocus blooms – the flowers last about three weeks – the stigmas are picked by hand, then dried in the sun and stored immediately in a sealed container so the aroma isn't lost. One fresh strand or three staler ones should be enough to flavour a pot of rice.

Shampoo

Chamomile shampoo

Make a cup of hot chamomile tea by pouring boiling water over a dessertspoon of dried chamomile flowers, leaving it to steep for five minutes. Drain the tea off the flowers and add a teaspoon of soap flakes – Lux is good – and a teaspoon of borax. Mix well. Use the whole cupful to wash your hair.

Chamomile tea by itself is a brightening rinse for fair hair.

Dry shampoo

Take orris root, ground rosemary, or arrowroot – by themselves, or in any combination. Orris root is the root of the Florentine iris – but I have also used the root of other irises with good effect. Dry them thoroughly in the oven, grind to a powder, and brush through your hair. Leave for ten minutes, then brush out again. The powder should take both grease and dirt with it.

Egg shampoo
Take the yolks of two eggs, add the juice of two lemons, mix, and use instead of shampoo.

Soap

This recipe produces a very soft soap, which hardens with age.

Wash 2 litres of water through 2 litres of wood ash – I use wattle ash or casaurina. Add about one litre of fat to the water and simmer until they emulsify. Chicken fat makes a very soft mixture; pig fat is said to make a harder one, but I haven't tried it.

Add perfume oils as the mixture cools down.

Scoop out spoonfuls of the soap as needed, or put it in an old 'liquid soap' dispenser.

Tea

The classic 'tea bush' is *Camellia sinensis*. It is a dense, shiny-leaved camellia with fragrant, single white or pale-pink flowers. It is a lovely shrub to grow even if you don't want to harvest tea. The Indian tea bush is also a camellia, *Camellia assamica*, and has similar requirements.

Tea is grown commercially in tropical monsoon areas. The bush can grow to an enormous size in the wild – up to 30 metres – but frequent harvesting keeps it trimmed to about 2 metres.

Tea bushes can be grown in any place in Australia which receives no more than light frosts and has a good supply of water. Any sheltered spot will do. The ideal temperature for good tea growth is between 20 and 30°C, but tea will tolerate more extreme conditions: we had a frost of minus 5°C this year, and the bushes were burnt a bit – that's all.

Choose a slightly acid, well drained soil with plenty of humus, or build up poor soil with mulch and compost. Tea bushes can be grown from seed or cuttings, usually the latter. The bushes are slow to grow in their early years – and may stagnate for about a year after planting – but then grow rapidly, especially in warm conditions. Start pruning the bushes after about three years to keep them in manageable size, and keep them well fed.

In subtropical areas you should be able to harvest tea from a three-year-old plant, though in colder areas it might be wise to wait anywhere up to five or even ten years, until the bush seems robust enough to stand regular trimming.

Harvesting tea

To harvest the tea, cut off the young leaves and dry them or use them fresh. In commercial production only the two top leaves and a bud are taken from every twig. Leaves are harvested every 9 days in winter to 21 days in summer, depending on the growth of the trees.

Different teas are made by treating the leaves in different ways. Black tea is made by piling the green leaves on the damp ground or on mats and letting them ferment before they are dried. Green tea, which is reputed to inhibit stomach and other cancers, is dried as soon as it is picked, and Oolong tea is semi-fermented.

Most tea drunk in Australia is black tea. If you can't develop a taste for green tea you will have to experiment with fermentation.

Common supermarket tea can be 'fragranced'by adding small quantities of herbs or blossom. Try adding some fresh or dried jasmine flowers for jasmine tea. Fresh or dried blossom is a delightful addition to a pot of tea, as is a twist of dried, but not crystallised, orange rind.

You can also extract a fragrant 'tea' oil from the tea seeds for use as a massage lotion or in cooking: pulverise the seeds in a blender, strain through some cheesecloth, and keep in a sealed bottle.

Toothpaste

Recipe 1

Take a small amount of orris root. This is the dried, ground root of Florentine iris – though other iris roots can be used too. Moisten with a little peppermint oil. This will clean your teeth well, but for children you might make the paste into something resembling commercial toothpaste: boil half a cup of pomegranate seeds in half a cup of water for twenty minutes, strain, and add to the paste.

This keeps for several weeks in the bathroom, or most of a year in the fridge.

Recipe 2

This is a good toothpaste, although it doesn't look like one.

Mix a tablespoon of dried sage leaves, dried rosemary leaves, orris root (see recipe 1), and arrowroot. Either dip the toothbrush into this powder as needed, or form a paste with quince gel and peppermint oil.

Turmeric

If you can buy a piece of fresh turmeric root, plant it. It grows like ginger, in a fertile, moist, well drained soil. Turmeric will die down in a frost – but as long as the root has developed well the previous season, it will shoot again, especially if it is protected with a thick layer of mulch to stop the ground from freezing, and providing the soil is well drained so the root doesn't rot.

Normally turmeric can be harvested ten months from planting. If you are growing it south of Brisbane, however, your root may take up to five years to become fleshy enough to harvest.

For home use, simply wash the roots well so that no grit adheres, then either use them fresh or boil them and dry them in a cool oven. Alternatively, preserve pieces fresh by covering them with olive oil.

Vanilla

While vanilla is a tropical crop, a substitute can be made by taking the strongly vanilla-scented leaves of vanilla grass and layering them with castor sugar, then using the sugar whenever vanilla flavour is needed. Vanilla grass is similar to lemon grass. It can be grown as an annual in cold areas – or taken inside in a pot during winter.

Wood polish

Simmer 1 cup of beeswax with three cups of olive oil. Allow to set. Rub in well.

Substitutes

Instead of garlic	Grow garlic chives: flat, thick chives, cold tolerant. Chop and use as needed.
	Grow garlic leeks: these are like thick garlic chives, as thick as small leeks. Grow them from seed, then let the clumps increase. Pull up what you need.
	Society garlic: this is a small hardy bush. Chop the leaves finely.
Instead of onions	Grow chives. Chop when needed. Siberian chives are produced in colder weather than ordinary chives, which die down in winter.
	Grow shallots. These aren't spring onions: they grow from a bulk, die down in winter, tolerate cold and are much more delicately flavoured than spring onions. Grow lots.
	Spring onions. Don't pull these up – just use the tops.
	Welsh onion. These are perennials with fleshy bases instead of bulbs. Use the tops or the bases too.
Instead of pepper	Tasmanian or native pepper which tolerates mild frosts but needs moist soil until established. Grind the dried seeds like pepper.
	Pepper tree, but use the leaves not the fruit. Dry the leaves and crumble them for a mild pepper flavour.
	Stonecrop: the juice of some stonecrops tastes peppery.
Instead of tea	Try the herbal teas till you find one you like: rose hip (collect your own), camomile (fresh camomile is infinitely better than dried, which tastes to me like compost), lemon balm, lemon grass, ginger mint, apple mint, hibiscus flower, or jasmine.

Instead of cloves	Carnations or dianthus – both are clove scented. Steep them in sugar, honey or brandy to transfer the flavour.
Instead of vanilla	Vanilla lily. It needs sun and moist soil. The flowers are pink to mauve on a long stalk and strongly vanilla scented. Steep them in sugar for vanilla sugar.
	Or grow vanilla grass: it grows like lemon grass and tolerates mild frosts.
Instead of sweet potatoes	New Zealand kumeras, which are frost resistant, small and good. Buy tubers at any good fruit store and plant them in spring. Keep them weed free. Kumeras aren't a sweet potato, though they are called that – they are really a form of oxalis.
Instead of lemons	Bush lemons or citronelles, which will take minus 5°C. They are rough, thick-pithed, full of seeds and slightly sweeter than most lemons.
	A Meyer lemon in a pot – take it indoors in winter.
	Lemon balm or lemon verbena. Neither give you lemon juice, but you can store them in sugar or brandy to transfer the flavour, or make a lemon-scented tea or cordial.
	Lemon grass on the window sill in cold areas. Add a little to curries, or make lemon essence by soaking it in brandy.
Instead of oranges	Seville oranges, which are bitter but cold tolerant.
	Valencia oranges, which are more cold tolerant than navels.
	Kumquats: modern kumquat varieties are sweet, as large as a child's fist, and delicious. They are also frost tolerant.
Instead of sugar cane	Sugar beet or even beetroot: red coloured sugar beet. Boil the beets and use the sweet syrup in cooking.
	Sugar maples. You can tap the sap from these in late winter where you have warm fine days, and nights cold enough for the trees to colour in autumn. Boil the sap till it thickens.
	Silverbirch: the sap from silver birch can be tapped and boiled like that of the sugar maple.
Instead of wheat flour	Replace one-third of the flour you would normally use in your recipes with cold, mashed potato.
	Dry potato or pumpkin and grind it to flour.
	Substitute one-third ground nuts – bunya or almond meal – for flour.
	Grind corn for cornflour, or dried beans for bean flour.
Instead of milk	Soak ground almonds or soybeans in water for a non-dairy milk – a little sweetening may be needed.
Instead of ginger	Grow ginger mint (good in ginger beer and stir-fried food), or ginger-scented pelargoniums (geraniums).
Instead of cinnamon, nutmeg, or mixed spice	Grow cinnamon-scented pelargoniums (geraniums): dry the leaves and crumble them to a cinnamon, spice or nutmeg powder.

Chapter 10

The backyard
medicine chest

Many of the minor complaints that we treat with remedies from the chemist – minor coughs, headaches, pimple cures, and the like – can also be treated with common plants from the backyard. In fact, most garden plants have a medicinal use – partly because our ancestors experimented with what they had, and also because many plants originally grown for their medicinal use now linger simply as ornamentals.

Only a few of the more common medicinal plants are listed here, in remedies for complaints that anyone can diagnose. When in doubt, seek medical advice.

Abrasions

Clean well. Wash either with warm water, or with a wash made by steeping comfrey root, calendula flowers, pomegranate or plantain leaves – or a mixture of them all – in a little boiling water. Use the liquid after straining. This wash can be kept in the fridge for use when needed.

Silverbirch sap, lavender oil or tea-tree oil can also be used as an antiseptic wash. Comfrey or witch-hazel ointment is excellent. If the abrasions become infected, soak them in warm water to which tea-tree oil has been added; then dry thoroughly. Repeat this three times a day.

Comfrey ointment

Clean and chop 50 g comfrey roots and steep in 500 Ml olive oil over low heat for 2 hours. Don't boil. Take off the heat – don't strain – and add 50 Ml melted beeswax.

Witch-hazel ointment

This is also good against aches, sprains or sunburn.

Steep 1 cup of the flowering twigs, leaves and bark in 2 cups of hot oil for

mortar & pestle

about 2 hours. Don't boil. Take off the heat, and add a dessertspoonful of melted beeswax. This can be left out if you just want to have a soothing oil handy to rub on aches and sprains or sunburn.

Bad breath

Pour 1 cup of boiling water over half a cup of peppermint leaves, fennel seed, and parsley. Gargle, rinse your mouth out – and drink the rest.

Burns

Use a cold compress or ice, as soon as possible, for as long as possible. Smear on chickweed juice if the skin is not broken. Smear on comfrey jell or the jell from aloe vera or prickly-pear leaves.

Colds

Sleep, relaxation, and drinking lots of water are the best cold cures available.

Try some kickagerm juice if you can stand it: mix two chopped cloves of garlic, half a teaspoon of grated ginger, the juice of a lemon, and a sprinkle of cinnamon in warm water, and drink it every three hours.

To help against fever, take an infusion in boiling water of equal parts of elder flowers, bergamot leaves, peppermint leaves and half as much yarrow: drink one cup with a clove of raw garlic, every three hours.

Coughs

Apart from eating a fresh clove of garlic four times a day, sucking candied horehound in honey stems as cough lollies, and sprinkling eucalyptus oil on your pillow at night, sip:

- Japanese menthol mint tea (excellent)
- horehound tea
- coltsfoot tea
- a teaspoon of the juice obtained by steeping a cut onion in honey
- an infusion of thyme, peppermint, coltsfoot, angelica leaves and root, and mullein leaves
- prickly-pear juice

To make an effective inhalation, infuse in boiling water some Japanese menthol mint leaves, mullein leaves, euphoria leaves, lungwort and hyssop (or any one of them, depending on what can be obtained); add a little eucalyptus or tea-tree oil; and inhale the steam.

Cradle cap

Bring 1 cup of chamomile flowers almost to the boil in some olive oil. Take it off the heat, cool and strain. Rub the oil gently onto the scalp, then wash it off with warm soapy water.

Dandruff

Rinse hair with nettle or rosemary tea or both. Wash with a raw egg instead of shampoo in case of allergy. Rinse hair with cider vinegar to remove residues that might irritate the scalp. Cover burdock root with boiling water, and use this as a rinse.

Nettle dandruff wash

Pour 1 cup of boiling water onto 1 cup of nettle leaves or roots. Leave until cool, strain, and rub into the scalp every day.

Eczema

Smear on fresh chickweed or watercress juice before any blisters form. When blisters do form, don't smear on anything that leaves a residue.

Eye strain

Pour boiling water over raspberry leaves, chamomile flowers, or elder flowers. Strain when cool, and bathe eyes with the lotion.

Flu

Take equal parts of elder flowers, peppermint leaves and half as much yarrow, and cover with boiling water. Drink one cup every three hours with a clove of raw garlic. Drink clear vegetable soup. Sip herbal tea throughout the day to replace fluid.

Headache

Headaches can have many causes. Frequent, severe, or prolonged headaches need professional diagnosis. For sinus headaches, see 'colds'. Take elderberry flower tea against fever headaches. For migraines, take cowslip and/or feverfew tea every two hours for twenty-four hours – but don't interrupt your sleep. Feverfew tea is made from both the leaves and flowers: 1 tablespoon to 3 cups of boiling water. Leave until cool.

Lavender tea is better for tension headaches. It is made from half a cup of flower heads steeped in boiling water, and can be sipped until the symptoms ease. Catnip tea, which is made from catnip leaves, is good against nervous headaches.

Generally, you could also try lavender oil applied to the temples.

Headache tea

Pour 2 cups of boiling water over 1 part sage leaves, 1 part rosemary leaves, 1 part yarrow leaves, 1 part lavender flowers, and 1 part peppermint leaves. Steep until cool enough to drink and take half a cup every hour – though not more than three cups a day.

Indigestion

Drink peppermint, lucerne, caraway or dill tea with a touch of anise or ginger to taste. Drink dandelion coffee after a rich meal. Try chewing a piece of liquorice root after meals to increase saliva.

Insect bites

Wash stings in vinegar as soon as possible; apply aloe vera jell, or St John's wort leaves.

The juice of young bracken stems is excellent for ant bites, while the juice of dock leaves or nettle stems is good for nettle rash.

If stings itch later, dab on alcohol: anything from brandy to listerine.

Insomnia

Valerian tea is relaxing and slightly bitter – try adding some honey. It is made by steeping the dried root in boiling water for 12 to 24 hours. Drink it cold. To dry the roots: dig them up, wash them, split them into quarters, and dry them in a dry, dark place before placing them in an airtight container. Valerian roots are slow to dry and may have to be left out for up to a year.

Itching rashes

Simmer 1 cup of chickweed in half a cup of olive oil for half an hour. Cool, strain and apply.

Laryngitis

Take 1 dessertspoonful of thyme, 1 dessertspoonful of chopped coltsfoot leaves and cover with 1 cup of boiling water. Leave for 5 minutes, add 1 teaspoon of honey, and use it warm as a gargle.

Nappy rash

Take 1 cup of chamomile flowers and 1 cup of elder flowers. Cover with boiling water, leave until cool, and strain. Wash the rash area with this whenever the nappy is changed.

Nausea

Take:
- lemon verbena tea,
- lavender tea,
- one teaspoon of half ginger and half honey,
- Chinese dried plums dusted with powdered ginger, or
- an infusion of chamomile flowers and mint leaves with a touch of cinnamon, cloves or ginger to taste.

Sore throat

Gargle every half hour with warm water with a little lemon juice, or with warm coltsfoot tea or witch-hazel tea. Or gargle with warm water with a touch of wintergreen oil. Or use a tea made with boiling water and blackberry leaves. Or make a tea with warm jullein or lavender – or use a combination of these.

Witch-hazel tea

Pour 1 cup of boiling water over 1 dessertspoonful of fresh leaves. Strain after 1 minute and gargle.

Sunburn

Apply:
• calendula ointment
• the juice of the calendula flower with a little nettle juice added if available
• sliced cucumber
• the juice of aloe vera leaves
• the juice of prickly-pear leaves
• mesembrythanthemum juice.

Toothache

Chew cobbler's pegs.

Warts

Wipe on marigold sap every night and morning, the milky sap of figs or dandelions twice a day, or fresh elderberry juice three times a day.

Chapter 11

A house for self-sufficiency

I'm writing this book on a Macintosh computer run by solar power. Solar power gives us our light and our (recorded) music, it runs most of our tools, the radio, printer, icecream machine, hair dryer, a 12-volt iron, video, blender, etc. Our total power costs are far lower than if we were connected to the grid – but we designed our lives to use less power. Generally this has been a comfortable adaption, although occasionally a guest's electric blanket or some tool won't run.

Solar power is cheap and effective – and the system can be added to as more power is needed, or you have more money to spend. To top up our power supply, we also run a small hydro system off the garden hose, and there's a water wheel down at the creek as well. Both are home-made and cost almost nothing: Bryan designed them and scavenged the materials.

This isn't the place to go into detail about a backyard alternative energy system – that would take another book – except to say it's possible, and it's fun. (Every sunny day you watch the panels charging up your batteries you think 'that's all for us'.) Whether it's appropriate for you is another matter. Most houses are already connected – expensively – to the grid, and it may not be worthwhile coping with another set of costs for an alternative system when you've already paid for one.

But if you do feel like producing your own power, it's even more rewarding than growing your own tomatoes.

Buildings

We live in an 'owner built' home: in other words, part was built by me, part by Bryan, and other bits by many friends. The base is stone from the creek below.

Anyone with two working hands can build their own home. (I know a paraplegic and a one-armed man who have done just that.) I can scarcely rule a straight line – but I can build a stone wall as long as I put up the formwork first.

Houses can be built of stone, rammed earth, mud brick, adobe (mud padded onto wattle branches or old chicken mesh), and roughly dressed home-grown timber. You can even make rammed earth floors, or fitted stone floors, or parquet wood floors, or even sand-and-cow-blood floors sealed with oil and wax. All of this can be 'free'. (Nothing is really free: what you don't buy you have to work for, and self-made houses take time instead of money.)

But a self-made house leaves you richer – not just in the money you haven't spent, but in the millions of memories. Every stone in this house has some association: the laughter and the fury and the hymn-singing competition we had when we rendered the kitchen, and how Jane sat reading to us from a book of etiquette she'd found at the dump while looking for an old tank for the woodshed – every time I look at that bit of wall I remember that you should never ask the Queen a direct question.

Self-made houses fit your needs – and your fantasies. They never stop growing. They're never finished either. One day we'll build that room with the fountain at the end. (It'll help the natural air conditioning.) Maybe one day Edward will really build his Norman tower at the end of his bedroom. Maybe one day we'll get round to putting down the skirting along the bathroom passage.

There is a house round here (3 bedrooms, large bathroom, dining room, etc.) built for $40 – the occupants scavenged the material by taking contracts to demolish old houses. Other houses grow gradually – the 'shells' are made from cheap or free materials like stone or pisé, the interiors are gradually finished as money becomes available. It's slow – but you don't need a mortgage, and it's much more fun.

It is not hard to do any of these things – to install your own power system, build your house, design your water system. All you need is the confidence to try – and the ability to laugh and try again – and a love of doing things for yourself, and enjoy it.

Making do

If anyone is uncertain about the way their life is going, I suggest they keep a diary. Not of the 'fed the ducks; caught train at 8 o'clock' variety, but one to record, every night, the most vivid and rewarding experiences of the day. These are usually simple – perhaps a paragraph you've read, the mist on the river, the scent of the wind, a conversation or just an exchange of laughter with a friend.

Do this for a month. Then read it back, and work out what are the most important things in your life: the things which really give you pleasure, really fulfil you – and what is just waste: things made and done to fill an empty life.

Someone once defined happiness as the right to spend extremely long hours doing something you love. If you count the minutes, you're doing the wrong thing.

Lives can be created. Work out what you love – and fill your life with it. Don't live second-hand via TV and video. Don't let other people's rules keep you to a job you hate, living in a house which is only tolerable. Every part of your life should give richness, or it's wasted – a house should be a place you love, not something to keep off the rain; a garden should be a place of fascination (what will bloom or fruit today, what bird will visit) instead of just a lawn, to mow on Sunday afternoons and to make your house identical with all the others in the neighbourhood.

This is what self-sufficiency is about: not just producing your own food to save money (though it will), or having an insurance policy in case civilisation collapses even further. It is about making your life richer, not just in material things, but in the memories and joy that can come with them.

Calendar

This calendar is based on the climate where I live: first frost in May, last in October, down to minus 5°C in winter. Sydney and Perth can plant things about one month earlier than we can; Melbourne about three weeks later; Brisbane about two months earlier, except in frost hollows; Adelaide about two weeks earlier (the Adelaide Hills are about the same as here, though); and Canberra and Hobart about three weeks later.

No matter where you are, if you're below the tropics the seasons change in much the same way. Use this chapter as a guide to the way the year can flow for you.

January

It's hot. The air smells of ripe peaches, the strawberries are rotting because you're sick of them, and you've still got a hangover from the dandelion champagne at Christmas. The last thing you want to do is plant your garden.

Unfortunately, after spring, January is the year's main planting time. Things you plant now will feed you from autumn to spring – and as nothing much grows during winter, you have to get things in now for them to mature in time. Take heart though – you don't have to dig: see Chapter 3 for minimum work gardens.

Plant	Winter crops like cauliflower, cabbage, broccoli, brussels sprouts, peas, and collards; in warm areas you can still plant small cucumber melons, and bush pumpkins. Plant Tom Thumb tomatoes in a pot to bear through winter.
	Anything planted now will take advantage of the autumn flush as it matures. The autumn flush really does exist, just like the spring flush: a sudden burst of plant growth that seems to have no direct correlation with temperature or moisture levels. Plant all the cabbage, cauliflower, broccoli, etc. you need for winter and spring.
Plant more	Beans as soon as the last lot start flowering; corn when the last lot reaches ankle high; and lettuce, carrots, silver beet, cabbage and potatoes. Plant more zucchini in case the first planting gets mildew (strongly growing young plants are more resistant). Also plant a new lot of tomatoes or take cuttings from old ones.
Harvest	You should be able to start picking the crops you planted in spring now: corn, tomatoes, beans, and zucchini. January is the bountiful time: it's as though nature cons you into planting more by showing you how wonderful the harvest can be.
	Wheat and oats should be ripening now. Don't let them get too ripe if you

are hand harvesting them, or they may shatter and you'll lose some of the grain.

Fruit   Late cherries, peaches, nectarines, plums, late apricots, early apples like gravenstein, passionfruit in warmer areas, mulberries, gooseberries, early grapes, early almonds, cape gooseberry, valencia oranges, lemons, avocados, babaco, pawpaw or mountain pawpaw in warm areas, strawberries, mid-season raspberries, loganberries, fruit from flowering prunus – good for jam, red, white and black currants, blueberries, banana passionfruit, mangoes in hot areas.

Pests   Check apples every week for signs of codling moth. Pick any tunnelled ones. Feed them to the chooks, stew them if they're ripe enough, or leave them under water for about three weeks.

Fruit fly   Remember that fruit fly are attracted to ripe fruit and mostly breed on the ground: pick all fruit just before it gets ripe, and never leave windfalls more than a day. Watch out for fruit fly breeding in 'compost heaps'. See *Natural Control of Garden Pests* (Jackie French, Aird Books) for details of organic fruit-fly control.

28-spot ladybirds   These like potatoes, tomatoes, and pepinoes. They speckled our eggplant leaves brown last year before I noticed what was happening. A reflective mulch (like aluminium foil or reflective insulation) will repel them. Masses of yellow daisies or marigolds will keep the numbers down as long as they are thickly planted underneath the other plants. I found last year that a strong nettle spray (nettles left in water till it turns brown – spray the dark brown liquid) helped repel them. As a last resort, make a spray of derris and water and spray it on the leaves – underneath as well. This is a stomach poison, not a contact poison: the ladybirds have to eat the leaf underneath to be affected. It will also repel them. For a long-term solution, attract birds and keep cats away.

Fruit rot   Try, weekly, a seaweed, a nettle, or even a weed spray. The best I know is a mixture of chamomile flowers, chives, nettles, seaweed, casuarina leaves, horsetail and comfrey – or as many of those as you can get. Cover with water and spray on foliage when the liquid is light brown. Spray just before picking, to minimise post-harvest rot. Thin out fruit if necessary. After picking, try and keep fruit as cool as you can: hot and humid storage areas, even for a short time, can start them rotting. Pick out any bad fruit at once. You can also try dipping fruit for a second or two into boiling water, or in hot, very salty water or hot chamomile tea. But make sure the fruit is dry before it's stored – I leave them to dry on newspaper.

Whitefly   If your plant leaves are mottled or speckled, look underneath for clouds of small white flies. Spray them thoroughly underneath the leaves every second day – and increase the potash in your soil with wood ash, comfrey, and compost.

February

February is the time you catch your breath. The holidays are over, and so is Christmas. You can plant all the things you didn't get round to last month, and start bottling the tomatoes.

Plant   The winter crops listed for January – though in cool or cold areas these may now not mature until spring – and spinach, which goes to seed in hot weather.

Plant more   Lettuce, and potatoes in warm areas or, in cold or temperate areas, in tyre gardens.

Harvest   Much the same as for January. Late maturers like capsicum and eggplant will be ripening now. Stick large pumpkins on a hot roof, to harden them. Onions planted last winter for storage should be lifted now, when the tops die off. Leave the dug onions in the sun for a couple of days to dry off, but don't let them get wet. Either hang them up in bunches by the dry tops or stick them in old orange netbags to make sure the air can circulate. Store them in a cool, dry, not necessarily dark place.

Don't bother if you can't eat everything that's ripe in the garden: February always provides too much. Remember that in the self-sufficient garden nothing is wasted: those surplus lettuces will make good mulch. Don't try and eat zucchini with every meal: throw them in the compost instead.

Apples start to crop well now – that is, the ones like Jonnies and Delicious that will store a few months, unlike the early apples that must be eaten straight from the tree or they taste floury.

Fruit   Brambleberries, raspberries, peaches, nectarines, plums, apricots, apples, passionfruit, mulberries, gooseberries, cape gooseberries, hazelnuts, almonds, grapes, figs, babaco, pepino, pawpaw or mountain pawpaw in warm areas, orange, lemon, avocado, strawberry guavas, strawberries, pears, early melons, brambleberries, tamarillos, and banana passionfruit.

Other jobs   Plant out strawberry runners. This is a good time for summer pruning, especially vines like kiwi fruit now the fruit has set. (Summer pruning's other name is 'hacking back the jungle'.) Bending back unwanted growth now will check plants far less than a rigourous pruning in winter, and cuts will heal quicker. If you must prune apricots or cherries, do so now.

Pests   At the first sign of powdery or downy mildew, pull off the infected leaves and compost or burn them. Make sure the soil is well mulched to stop contact between vines and damp soil – and any leaf residues in the soil. Spray with chamomile tea or milk if the infestation is light, otherwise with half-strength bordeaux. Spray under the leaves as well, and on top of the mulch where spores may linger.

Have another crop coming on elsewhere in the garden too: younger, strongly growing plants will be less stricken, and you'll extend your cropping even if you don't spray.

March

March is the harvest month: the time to gather in what you have grown and keep safe for winter. It's a gentle month. The sun isn't as fierce and there's a touch of lushness in the growth: the autumn flush before the winter.

The weather is cooling now. With a few exceptions like spinach, broad beans, and cabbages the main vegetable planting time is over.

Plant   Spinach in warm areas; early onions; lots of cabbages of different sizes: early, small ones may mature by winter, others will mature in spring. Early broad beans put in now may get aphids: just pinch off the aphid infested tops, wash them, steam them, and eat them.

Harvest   Tomatoes will be glutting now. Melons and okra will be ripening. Test melons for ripeness by sniffing them, (a fruity smell indicates ripeness) and by tapping them to see if they sound hollow. As well as most summer vegetables, early cabbages and other winter vegetables may be starting to mature. This is a good time for peas, and for digging sweet potato roots.

Don't pick pumpkins till the stems turn dry near the base of the pumpkin, then let them 'cure' or harden for a week or two on a hot roof or on dry cement. This will help stop them rotting in late winter. Pumpkins that aren't quite ripe will still be sweet – but they won't store well.

Fruit
Olives, oranges, lemons, kumquats, figs, late peaches, late nectarines, apples, passionfruit, pepino, babaco, pawpaw or mountain pawpaw in warm areas, sapote mulberries, hazelnuts, almonds, orange, lemon, tamarillo, strawberries, raspberries, brambleberries, early quinces, early persimmons, pears, melons, pecans, bunya nuts, late grapes, and banana passionfruit.

Other jobs
Plant more peas or broad beans for 'green manure': slash them in late winter or early spring just as they start to flower, to provide mulch and fertiliser for a no-dig garden.

Start to prepare for frost now: work out which trees are vulnerable, like avocados, citrus, and tamarillos, and start building shelters for them. See also Chapter 5.

Pests
Keep up fruit fly lures till there have been none caught for three weeks. Most pests will vanish as the weather cools down.

April

I love autumn: blue sky and purple shadows and a gentle, gold light. In autumn the soil cools down and things start growing. Autumn flushes are as marked as spring flushes. Fruit swells as much in a week as it did in the previous month and new soft shoots appear all over the place.

Don't clean up the garden. Leave those corn stalks, radish-going-to-seed and patches of weeds alone. The weeds probably won't seed or run about till spring anyway – and they'll protect the soil and help insulate your plants.

Gardeners who recommend you spend your peaceful winter months 'tidying up the garden' just have a fetish for straight rows and nice chocolatey, bare earth. This may help their spirits but it won't help the garden. Gardens are wasted on people with a passion for sweat and blisters. Gentle pottering and a bit of contemplation are more effective than maniacs with mattocks.

Plant
Autumn is the time to prepare for the hungry gap. The hungry gap is spring to early summer. It's the time when you have eaten most of the surplus from last autumn – the apples, pumpkins, old carrots and parsnips in the garden – but the new season's crops are still months away from maturing.

A few hundred years ago the hungry gap was the starvation time, the scurvy and plague time, when the weather was warming up but people's diet was still poor.

It's a bit late now for most things. Anything you plant now must either be quick-maturing, or the sort of plant that will go quickly to seed as soon as the weather heats up: like peas, cauliflowers, and broccoli – the sprouts and pods you eat are the immature seed heads. Plant to eat them in spring. Start putting in brown-skinned long-keeping onions now. If the soil is still warm enough to sit on, put in winter lettuce, winter radish,

Chinese mustard, kale, corn salad and swedes in temperate areas.

The carrots, celery, silver beet, etc. you planted last spring will have to last you to the next one, the pumpkins and melons ripening on the vine will be stored through winter, the cauliflower and other brassicas should be steadily maturing.

If you don't have enough crops in by now you will either be hungry or you'll have to go shopping at the supermarket in spring.

Harvest

All the 'year-rounders', Chinese cabbage, and the last of the summer vegetables.

In colder regions autumn is the harvest season, frantic with bottling. Where I live, most harvests are in summer. Autumn harvests are gentler: late apples, late pears, pomegranates, medlars, quinces. The fruit is full of summer sun without that almost frantic, fermented sweetness that crops get in high summer.

This is the time for gathering whatever will be spoiled by winter cold: green tomatoes to make into green tomato pickle, and immature cucumbers and pumpkin to slice and stir-fry.

Fruit

Pomegranates, medlars, Valencia oranges, lemons, early limes, olives, late figs, quinces, Granny Smith apples, passionfruit, tamarillos, late grapes, chestnuts, walnuts, persimmons, grapefruit, guava, feijoa, strawberry guava, late strawberries, raspberries, bananas, avocados, Irish strawberry-tree fruit, melons, and pecan.

Ripening immature vegetables

Pull up tomatoes, capsicum, vines, etc. with as much soil as possible. Hang them in a shed or under the verandah. The crop will continue to ripen.

Even green tomatoes will keep ripening on newspaper indoors – check for bad ones often. Don't dig root crops till you're going to use them – they'll be sweeter for the cold. If the ground may freeze, mulch over them or try to shelter them with tall plants around them. Move some potted plants next to them – I use a prolific climbing geranium in pots to protect small vulnerable plants.

Other jobs

This is the time to think about last minute seed saving. Transplant any carrots, parsnips, etc. which you may be saving for seed into a less used part of the garden should they be in the way where they are. Transplanting them now will only make them go to seed quicker. Stake them well: they'll get top heavy when the seed heads form and may fall down, causing the seed to rot or sprout prematurely.

Think about green manuring unused ground to prepare it for spring – clearing weeds, fixing nitrogen, and adding humus: lucerne, broad beans, peas, and field peas.

Pests

This isn't a bad time of year for pests: the great population explosions have come and gone, and predators should have built up to cope with the remnants.

If you have winter-maturing fruit keep up your fruit-fly traps and orchard hygiene. Otherwise just make sure that you don't have any old fruit in nice, warm, slowly decomposing compost heaps or pits: places where fruit fly can cozily over-winter.

Check any late-maturing apples like democrats or grannies or Lady Williams every few days for the sawdust-like deposits from codling moth larvae. If you find any pick off the apples and either feed them to the animals or stick them in a plastic bag to anaerobically compost over winter.

Remove any old ladders or boxes near the trees where codling moth can hibernate, pick up any windfalls or let the chooks do it for you.

If you're troubled by harlequin beetles in the garden – sometimes called 'push-me-pull-yous' because of their active sex lives – stick some broad pieces of cardboard on the ground around the garden. Check each afternoon for sheltering beetles. This should reduce the numbers in your garden considerably next season.

Stick hens or other animals under fruit trees and in the old tomato patches now if you can – they'll help clean up any fruit residues that might help fruit fly over-winter.

May

May is clear blue skies here. The air is cool, but the soil still warm. It's the time when you wait for the first frost to mark the beginning of winter.

Plant   Broad beans, long-keeping onions like pukahoe, and peas.

Don't be tempted by blue sky. Even if the soil still feels warm, any soft new growth may be frosted off. Stick to broad beans and other hardy plants that will mature in spring.

Harvest   Potatoes, year-rounders, and strip corn stalks for 'baby corn'. Root vegetables are good now after the first frost – much sweeter.

Potatoes should have been harvested by now – and another crop put in if you can grow them in above-ground beds of old tyres where they will get little frost.

Fruit   Early mandarins, limes, pomegranates, late apples, late Valencias or early navel oranges, tangelos, citrons, kumquats, tamarillos, early kiwi fruit, late passionfruit high up on the vine, late raspberries, late strawberries if grown on a high garden away from early frost, olives, persimmons if the birds haven't finished them, feijoa, bananas, avocados, banana passionfruit and other passionfruit high on the vine, elderberries, medlars, olives, melons, and guavas.

Other jobs Clean out green houses now, and leave them open to the sun for a time. Take shelves out to air, and wash them in disinfectant or vinegar if they may be harbouring fungus or disease spores.

Make use of a slow garden and warm weather to revamp the chook house for next spring's chickens; build a mobile hen run to keep down the grass; build more compost heaps; make pot pourri with the last of the rose petals and scented leaves before they are frosted.

Pests   This is a month of prevention. Prune off dead twigs, mummies, band apple trees with grease, corrugated cardboard or old wool to help control codling moth and oriental peach moth, and clean up old ladders and fruit boxes where moths may shelter. Let hens scavenge round the orchard to pick up old fruit or insects on the ground.

June

This is hibernating time. Humans huddle round hot drinks – pests like harlequin beetles, fruit fly, slugs and snails shelter in slow 'compost heaps' (really piles of weeds), ready to breed in spring. A good compost heap should be hot enough to kill pests. If it isn't, piss in it, or add another form of nitrogen until it does.

Thrips will be seeing the winter out on flowering weeds. When the weeds die off in spring they'll move to your plants. Either get rid of the weeds or, better still, plant more flowering ground covers round trees and along garden paths to tempt the thrips away from your fruit trees (thrips prefer to be close to the ground), and to attract early predators in spring.

Plant Onions; winter lettuce and other 'April crops' may be planted if the soil feels warm – but they'll mature just as fast planted in spring; plant crowns of rhubarb, asparagus; berry roots, Jerusalem artichoke tubers unless the ground freezes – in which case wait till spring.

Harvest Year-rounders; winter veg planted in January: cabbage, broccoli, brussels sprouts, cauliflowers, carrots, beetroot, winter lettuce, parsnips, swedes, turnips, foliage turnips, celery, broad bean tips, tampala, spring onions, collards, parsley, winter radish, spinach, and silver beet.

Winter storage Don't keep carrots near fruit: the skin may turn bitter as ethylene is released from the fruit. Don't store spuds with fruit either, especially apples, or they'll sprout earlier. If you can be bothered, wrap fruit in newspaper – it'll keep longer – or fill the fruit box with clean, dry sand. Root vegetables need some humidity or they'll wither. (Ever wondered why shop-bought carrots look lush while yours start to shrivel?) Keep them in plastic bags with air holes, or in damp sand. Tomatoes ripen best in crumpled newspaper – and if any of them rot, the newspaper will absorb the juice, so the rest won't be affected.

Beware of codling moth breeding in your apple store – more apples are infected with codling moth in storage than on the tree. It's worthwhile leaving small open jars of sweet port (or molasses and water if you have an alcoholic cat) near stored apples to trap the moths. Try pasting a few sheets of newspaper over the apple boxes to stop codling moth and fruit fly getting in.

Fruit Apples (Lady Williams), feijoa, navel oranges, kiwi fruit, limes, mandarins, citrons, grapefruit, bananas, avocados, late passionfruit high on the vine, banana passionfruit, guava, strawberry guava, medlars, olives, late tamarillos above the frost, and a very few late raspberries.

Pests Mid-winter is the classic time for preventive spraying with bordeaux against curly leaf (pinkish raised blisters on peaches and almonds), rust, shot hole (small holes in leaves, most common on apricots), brown rot (exactly that: a brown, soft rot on fruit, sometimes with a furry outside), black leaf spot, bacterial blight in walnuts, and other fungal and bacterial conditions.

July

This is the slow time of the year: the time to watch the garden through the window; to see where the frost falls and what bits get the sunlight first; to dream of what and where you'll plant when the shadows grow small again.

Plant Most seed sown in cold wet ground will rot. (It helps to coat it with salad oil before planting.) Most plants sown now won't do much until spring – and spring-sown plants will soon catch up with them anyway. Onions are still an exception though.

In warm areas, try potatoes in late July. They will take at least a month to shoot anyway, and by then days will be warmer. Try them in beds of old tyres (see Chapter 3).

Harvest	See June. Root vegetables are sweetest now, after frost and cold nights. Try them grated into salads with lots of parsley. Winter fruit will be at its best now, too – frost makes citrus softer and sweeter, and seems to give late Lady Williams apples a unique zing.
Fruit	Apples (Lady Williams), navel oranges, kiwi fruit, limes, mandarins, citrons, grapefruit, bananas, avocados, tangeloes, medlars, alpine strawberries, and cape gooseberries grown in a pot or sheltered spot.
Other jobs	Plant deciduous trees, rhubarb crowns, and asparagus. Daydream through seed and fruit tree catalogues, planning for next season. Clean up garden rubbish and make a final winter compost heap – and take a break.

August

This is a month to gird your loins and start dreaming of what you're going to do in spring. Don't try doing much yet. It's still too early.

Plant	Potatoes, peas, parsley, snow peas, radish and cabbages can be sown when the air is warm but the soil still cool. But coat the seeds in cooking oil to stop them rotting in cold soil. Dust them with white pepper after oiling if you're worried by snails. When the soil is warm enough to sit on bare-bummed, plant tomatoes, corn, silver beet, carrots, celery, capsicum, dandelions, eggplant, okra, Chinese mustard, melons, pumpkins, and zucchini.
Harvest	You'll still be picking the same old veg as last month – but there'll be more brussels sprouts, cauliflowers will be starting to form centres, and there'll be new shoots off the broccoli. Don't just pick the main bunch – keep picking all the little bits that follow. In warm areas you might just get the odd sprig of asparagus and a few broad beans. Start gorging on winter root vegies like carrots and beetroot now, before they go to seed when the weather warms up.

Also, early peas or snow peas plus year-rounders like carrots, radish, beetroot, silver beet, celery, turnips, foliage turnips, and parsnips; and winter veg like cabbage, cauliflowers, broccoli, brussels sprouts, collards, early dandelion leaves from last year's growth, spinach, and parsley. |
Fruit	Navel oranges, lemon, tangelo, mandarin, kiwi fruit, grapefruit, avocados, and limes.
Other jobs	Lay down weed mat for next month's gardens. Build no-dig beds. Don't be in a hurry to pull out last year's debris to make room for new crops: the debris will protect the remaining plants from late frost.
Pests	Clean up piles of rubbish. Douse them with hen manure or blood & bone and hope they turn into compost. Pick off all dried fruit mummies that may infect next season's crops.

September

Subduing those spring urges   Spring does strange things to gardeners. Maybe it's just the sap rising in the trees and the scent of blossom that send you out to plant things.

Don't: plants that are placed in cold soil never do as well as those planted when the soil warms up. Don't plant until the soil welcomes anything you put in: a cold bed and a cold welcome dismays plants as well as people. Tomatoes planted now will probably bear at about the same time as those planted six weeks later – but the later plantings will be sturdier and bear longer.

Pests attack early plantings. Most pests start breeding at about 3°C, while most predators only begin to be active at about 12°C. Wait till the world is ready to receive your bean seeds and capsicum plants – don't try to hurry spring along.

How do you know when to plant? One bit of folklore wisdom says to plant tomatoes when the soil is warm enough to sit on with bare buttocks. In suburban areas use the back of your wrist. Another old saying has you planting corn when the peach blossom falls. I do this every year, and it works – unless, of course, your peach blossom happens to be frosted off.

On the other hand, there is the 'spring flush'. This really exists: spring-grown crops grow faster than ones planted later. You just have to use your judgment – get plants in early enough to catch the spring tides, but not so early that they're stunted or frosted off.

Plant See August. The next three months are the main planting time for the year. You're planting the things you'll eat all summer, as well as many of the things you'll be eating through autumn, winter, and hopefully next spring as well. Many crops like silver beet, celery, leeks, spring onions, parsley, beetroot, carrots, parsnips, turnips, and foliage turnips can all be planted in one go to see you through the year. If you're short of room, however, you can plant them over the next few months as space becomes available. These are the 'year-rounders', the crops you'll rely on as the foundation of your vegie garden all year round. Other crops, like pumpkins and watermelons, are also one-crop plantings: plant enough to pick and store.

Then there are the staggered croppers: beans, lettuce, peas, corn, tomatoes, and zucchini. I tend to plant a new succession when the first lot is just starting to flower. It works better than planting every two weeks as, especially early in the season, early and late planted crops tend to catch up with each other and you end up with a glut.

Quick maturers Early summer can be a lean time when you're living from your garden: last year's plants have gone to seed and the next lot are still too young to eat. Try some of the old peasant stand-bys. Luckily we have a lot of peasant cultures to choose from: Australian 'backyard peasants' can have a much more varied diet than any traditional peasant ever dreamed of.

Radish Round red ones are ready in about one month and the leaves can be snipped for salads or steamed after two weeks – more will re-grow. If, like me, you don't like raw radish, try cooking them – they taste a bit like asparagus.

Chinese mustard Also called Chinese spinach or Bok Choi, this can be eaten small and young – again, in the same way you'd use spinach or lettuce. It's a very fast grower but resists running to seed when it gets hot.

Tampala or Chinese spinach This is another fast grower. Use it as soon as you can bear to pick the leaves. The plant will eventually grow to about one metre tall, when you just eat the leaf tips. Tampala is very tender and delicate – much more delicate than silver beet, and it suits even conservative eaters.

Baby carrots like Amsterdam forcing Don't thin them – just pull them as soon as they're big enough.

Cos lettuce Just pull off individual leaves as soon as they are big enough, without pulling up the lettuce, so the rest eventually hearts. You can do the same with Prizehead Red: simply harvest a bit whenever you have a salad. Rocket also gives quick salads, but it is a bit pungent and smoky for some tastes. Try soaking it in milk overnight before serving.

Cut celery   A celery used like parsley, very strongly flavoured. Seed can be sown all year round throughout Australia.

Rocket   Also called rucca or *Eruca sativa*, it can be sown all year round – it self-sows with vigour. Steam the young leaves or eat them in salads. The older leaves are slightly bitter and smoky – loved by some, but not by me.

Purslane   An annual sown in spring in cool conditions, and all year round in tropical to subtropical areas. Cook it or eat it raw. Cut the leaves at 10 cm high or less, when they're soft and tender.

Watercress   You can be eating this in a month, but beware of tiny snails which carry liver fluke: wash even home-grown watercress in three changes of water.

Silver beet   You should have your first picking in a month if you feed and water them well.

Chinese cabbage   Don't try this in subtropical areas: it'll bolt to seed unless you grow it in a cool, shaded place. In cooler areas you may be picking it two months from planting.

Harvest   All-rounders and winter veg may start to go to seed. Pick out seed heads regularly to delay them. Mulch heavily to keep the soil cool. This will also delay vegies going to seed. Pick broccoli every day so it doesn't toughen or go to seed – feed and water it well. Leave your cauliflower plants in the ground after you've picked them: they may produce new, smaller hearts, a bit like pale broccoli.

Every year I bless the time I put in asparagus and artichokes – they are the first real sign of spring. It's ironic that when fresh veg are scarcest, two of the most wonderful crops appear in abundance.

Hungry-gap crops   See also under April. Now that we can get golf ball tomatoes and pineapples any time of the year, a lot of the old spring foods have been forgotten. Most people won't eat or harvest anything they don't recognise from the supermarket – and most of us now prefer much blander foods. Bitter food was presumed to be a spring tonic in both European and Asian folklore.

Many traditional 'hungry gap' foods are all good, if now unconventional. Try them before you reject them. If you baulk at eating prickly pear fruit, mistletoe jam or carrot tops, remember that it's better than an elderly, well-travelled tomato, that wasn't much good in the first place.

Flowers   It may be a coincidence, but a lot of the early spring flowers are edible. Flowers are high in both vitamins (especially vitamin C) and minerals: an advantage when a lot of the vitamins had vanished from long-stored spring food.

Weeds   While many weeds are edible most of the year, they are only really good in early spring. After that their leaves get tough and bitter.

Winter leftovers   Many vegetable bits that we discard are as good as the main crop. Look for:

Cabbage stalks   These should be peeled of their tough skin, steamed, and served like asparagus.

Brussels sprouts or broccoli leaves   Shredded and stir-fried, they are also good with sauteed apples in butter.

Leeks going-to-seed   Cut off the seed stalk, peel it, and chop it into any vegetable dish.

Carrots going-to-seed   Grate them down to the tough core, slice it off, then grate the rest. Or add grated tough carrots to egg and wheat germ to make dog biscuits.

Celery going-to-seed   Cut out and peel the seed head. Serve it finely sliced, like cucumber.

Brussels sprout leaves   Try them shredded and stir-fried like cabbage.

Eating immature vegetables

Carrot tops   Chop them finely, like celery.

Young celery leaves

Broad bean tips   Steam them like silver beet. This is also a good remedy if they've got aphids.

Globe artichoke stalks   Peel and steam them.

Beetroot leaves   Eat them like silver beet. Don't use sugarbeet leaves or golden beet leaves: they can be poisonous.

Hop or choko shoots   Steam and serve with butter.

Zucchini or pumpkin flowers   Stuffed or butter-fried, these are also good dipped in batter and deep-fried.

Garlic leaves   Chop and add them to stews or salads.

Tiny radish leaves   Can be chopped and added to mashed potato, or dipped in batter and deep-fried.

Young sunflower or poppy leaves   Can be added to salads. But don't use too many unless you're also looking for a medicinal effect.

As for the rest of the garden: try adding young citrus leaves to salads or as a flavouring to custards; crumble dried avocado leaves and use them in stuffings for a rich avocado flavour; pluck bamboo shoots and boil them in salted water till tender; pickle broom buds or hibiscus buds like capers; tap a silver birch or manna gum for sweet sap; stew angelica or hibiscus stalks like rhubarb; bake green pawpaws; slice waterlilly stalks instead of cucumber; pickle tiny green apples or tiny citrus in a sweet pickle solution and eat them like olives; dig out bullrush roots and roast them like potatoes; and make tea from mints and herbs. You'll be foraging in the best harvest traditions of our ancestors.

Fruit

Navel oranges, lemons, limes, tangelo, mandarin, avocado, small alpine strawberries (not the large new varieties that fruit later), cape gooseberries if they haven't been frosted off (autumn's will mature now), ditto tamarillos, and rhubarb.

Stopping plants go to seed

Mulch heavily while the ground is still cold.

Pick out the long 'hearting' stalks as soon as they form. (Eat them: most are tender and sweet.) Dig up left-over root vegetables like carrots and beetroot before they toughen. Store them wrapped in newspaper away from fruit. This will help send them to seed even out of the garden. They will gradually shrivel, but shrivelled carrots and beetroot often taste sweeter than plump ones. Don't judge them till you've had a bite.

Other jobs

Just keep planting. The rest can wait.

Pests

Spring is pests' big chance: few predators and lots of soft, sappy growth. Try not to water spring crops, and don't fertilise them till the spring flush is over – and never give high-nitrogen fertiliser.

A heavy mulch now will not only slow down spring growth, but also slowly release the nutrients that your plant will need through the year. No, I'm not crazy: a heavy mulch will cut down both on the danger of late frost and on pest attacks – and the plant will more than catch up later. It also keeps down weed competition, encourages earthworms, and stops moisture loss.

Let some vegetables go to seed and let them flower around your garden. This is perhaps the most important spring advice there is: flowering vegetables are one of the best ways to attract pest-eating predators. Most adult predators eat nectar from flowers; only their offspring are carnivorous. Happily, most prefer the nectar from the plants their offspring like to forage over for pests: your vegies.

Letting vegetables go to seed will also give you a stock of home-grown seed for next year – fungicide free and suited to your area.

October

This is the exciting time: trees are setting fruit, and are bright with pale-green leaves – it's a time to dream about the abundance to come in a couple of months. October is just too encouraging. The days are balmy, and you feel like you can cultivate the world.

Take a grip on yourself. Whatever you plant now you'll have to tend at Christmas. Three dozen tomatoes planted now mean one week bottling or freezing or saucemaking in late summer; three zucchini plants will mean you're forcing them on your friends. The more you dig now the more you'll have to weed in a month's time.

Start small, and extend your plot week by week. That way you won't start more than you can tend. Don't dig either. Sometimes I think humans have a sort of instinctive urge to dig – like kids digging in a sandpit. Dig if you must, but don't assume it'll make your garden any better – try a no-dig garden instead (see Chapter 3).

Plant See August. Cool areas will start spring planting now. In warmer areas, plant more lettuce, beans and corn.

Harvest Like September, this is a month that tells you how good your garden planning was last year. We'd have had peas if the wallaby hadn't eaten them, and young dandelion leaves if the wombat hadn't sat on them. (The leaves are probably still edible but I don't fancy them.) Keep picking the tops out of silver beet that goes to seed so they'll keep cropping till the new lot are ready. Pick brussels sprouts as soon as they form, so more grow. Asparagus will be yielding now, and early artichokes. In warm areas lettuce, Chinese spinach, corn salad and peas may be starting to yield, if planted in August.

Fruit Loquat, navel orange, lemon, lime, tangelo, mandarin, avocado, early strawberries, very early raspberries in warm areas, rhubarb, banana passionfruit, and tamarillos ripening from last season.

Other jobs Broad beans don't set seed in hot weather: mulch them thickly now to keep the soil cool. If they start getting spots on their leaves you've probably got a potash deficiency: throw wood ash on the plot, for next year. Let excess or old broad beans dry in the pod – then keep them to add to soups and stews later.

Chop up vegies gone-to-seed and stew them into a rich vegetable stock – either have it for lunch or freeze it. A friend grates them, adds wheat germ, and bakes them into crisp dog biscuits.

Many veg, like carrots and celery, that have gone to seed can be eaten simply by peeling away the tough outer membrane: the centres will be soft and sweet.

Plant green-manure crops that can be slashed and ready for January plantings of winter vegetables: broad beans (cut them at flowering, don't wait for pods to set) or sunflowers, buckwheat or even radish if you pull them out before the bulbs form.

Mulch strawberries and rhubarb now, and cut off any rhubarb heads going to seed. Mulching now prevents leaf disease later.

Buy young chooks now: they'll lay through to next spring. If you don't raise your own chickens, try buying black, white and red ones alternately, to 'colour code' each year – or leave different colour roosters with the females each season.

If your chooks aren't laying well, check their water: fresh, running water means more eggs, while a stagnant puddle may keep your hens alive but they won't thrive. Hens won't lay in very hot weather either: scatter branches over the chook run for some shade, and plant some trees, preferably trees like mulberries, tree lucerne or avocados which can provide chook food.

Chooks are paranoid creatures. They can be scared of anything that flies over them and anything that chases them – from kids to foxes. Scared chooks don't lay well. Once, chooks were jungle birds, living in the broken light of the undergrowth. If you want secure, non-paranoid chooks, stick branches, old corn stalks, etc. over their run so that the light below is shifting and semi-shaded. They'll feel less vulnerable, no matter what is around.

Pests   No matter what pests are bugging you, try not to do anything about it for at least another two weeks – see if natural predators won't start doing the job for you.

November

Summertime, and the livin' is easy: gardens are starting to crop, trees are hanging heavy with fruit, the chooks are laying – and the weeds are poking their heads above the lettuces while your lawn is threatening to creep through the windows and choke you in your beds.

Well, I warned you about digging. Dug garden beds breed weeds. Next time, try no-dig methods (see Chapter 3) and re-plant the lawn with a useful 'no-mow' alternative – or plant asparagus there instead.

Plant   November is the time to evaluate what you've planted, and what you need to plant. Do you have enough carrots, parsnips, and celery to last a year? Have you put in enough tomatoes, watermelon and zucchini? Are you continuing to put in successions of corn, beans, and lettuce?

Plant more   Beans whenever the last lot flower; corn and lettuce every three weeks; radish every month; and cabbage whenever you remember. I usually stick in another lot of cucumbers and zucchini in December in case early plantings are hit by powdery mildew. Plant them well away from the first lot, with a tall crop like corn in between if you can. Plant another large lot of corn now too, so you have some to store for winter.

Harvest   Most winter crops and all-rounders will have gone to seed; broad beans and peas will be fruiting; early silver beet can be snipped small and young; mignonette lettuce sown in August will be ready; parsley will still be plentiful; dandelions will be leafy and sweet; and you can gorge on asparagus and artichokes.

Fruit	Cherries, early peaches, early nectarines, early apricots, small early plums, Joaneting apples (late November to December), loquat, orange, lemon, lime, grapefruit, strawberries, and raspberries.
	An easy way to pick cherries, if you're not going to store them, is to climb a tree with a pair of scissors and snip the bunches, then gather them at the bottom of the tree. This also tells the birds that the whole cherry tree territory is yours – not just the bottom branches. Otherwise they sit at the top of the trees and sneer at you.
Other jobs	Feed lettuce, seedlings, celery, silver beet and corn with liquid manure.
	Weeds are the worst problem now. Don't pull them out. Cover them with newspaper or with strips of weed mat weighted down with rocks. Feed your plants more while the weeds die and turn to fertiliser beneath their mulch.
	Annual weeds don't even need to be mulched. Whippersnip or mow them instead, then use the residue to mulch your plants. We get young oats springing up out of the mulch. Don't regard it as an enemy: turn the mulch over to suffocate it, or just keep snipping of the tops.
Pests	Start spraying fruit with chamomile tea or seaweed spray every week if your are worried about brown rot. Thin them out too, and keep bad ones picked off. Spray pear and cherry slug with derris or pyrethrum spray – or leave them alone if they're not killing the tree.

December

This is a month for minimising work. There are too many other things happening in December to concentrate on the garden. Just make sure you keep up successive plantings – beans and corn in particular – and that the garden doesn't quite disappear in the undergrowth. Don't bother weeding: just cut off the tips, or bury them under mulch.

Plant	See November. Keep up successive plantings of corn, beans and lettuce – but otherwise wait till Christmas is over and you get a chance to breathe.
Harvest	New potatoes planted in August; Tom Thumb tomatoes in warm areas or where they are pot grown; peas, silver beet, baby carrots, lettuce, tiny beetroot, celery tops, zucchini in warm areas, dandelions, bush pumpkins in warm areas or where they live have been started in pots; asparagus and artichokes in cool areas.
Fruit	Cherries, plums, peaches, apricots, Joaneting apples, nectarines, passionfruit, banana passionfruit, gooseberries, cape gooseberries, Valencia oranges left on the tree, lemons, strawberries, raspberries, loganberries, and sometimes early figs.
	Many pests – not just fruit fly – are attracted by the scent of overripe fruit, so keep harvesting: pick everything as soon as it's ripe, or a bit before. Fruit fly or codling moth fruit often do fall earlier. Never leave fallen fruit on the ground: call in the geese or chooks or do it yourself.
Pests	See November. However, with Christmas, and picking fruit and harvesting your garden, you probably won't have time.
	Concentrate on growing and picking things, and enjoy the bounty of your garden.

Index